Contents

ADULTING FOR COLLEGE STUDENTS

Essential Skills Your Parents Forgot to Teach You (and College Never Will) - Build Credit, Cook Real Meals, and Navigate Leases Without Calling Home for Help

EVE PARKER

Created with the assistance of AI tools and extensively edited and approved by the author.

Introduction

It was 2:17am on a Tuesday when Olivia found herself standing barefoot outside her student accommodation, keys glinting mockingly at her from the other side of the glass door. Her phone was at 3% battery, she had exactly $2.43 in her purse, and somewhere in the back of her mind, she remembered getting a text from her bank about "insufficient funds" that she'd ignored earlier that day.

This was the moment Olivia realized that being 19 years old didn't automatically come with an instruction manual.

Her first instinct? Call her parents. At 2am. Because surely they would know what to do about lockouts and overdrafts and why her debit card had stopped working at the corner shop. The conversation went something like this:

"Mom, I'm locked out and my card isn't working and I think I might owe the bank money and I don't know who to call or what to do and—"

"Sweetheart, slow down. Have you tried calling the accommodation office? And when did you last check your bank balance?"

"There's an accommodation office? And... how do I check my bank balance?"

If this sounds familiar, you're not alone. Olivia's 2am panic call represents a moment that happens to almost everyone: the sudden realization that nobody actually taught you how to be an adult.

They just expected you to figure it out.

Here's the truth that nobody talks about: the gap between being looked after and looking after yourself is enormous, and most of us are expected to leap across it without a safety net or a map. School taught you about quadratic equations and the causes of World War I, but somehow missed the bit about what to do when your landlord doesn't fix the heating, or how to build a credit score, or why you shouldn't just ignore those official-looking letters from the council.

Your parents probably tried their best, but there's a difference between knowing how to do something and knowing how to teach someone else to do it – especially when half the adult world has gone digital since they figured it out themselves.

This book exists to bridge that gap. Not with patronizing lectures about "responsibility," but with practical, step-by-step guidance for the stuff you need to know right now. It's the instruction manual that should have come with your 18th birthday, covering everything from "how to talk to your landlord without sounding like a child" to "what those numbers on your bank statement actually mean."

The goal isn't to turn you into a perfect adult overnight (spoiler alert: perfect adults don't exist). It's to give you the tools and confidence to handle everyday situations without panicking, make informed decisions about money and housing, and gradually build the life skills that will serve you for decades to come.

WHO THIS BOOK IS FOR

This book is written for anyone who's ever felt like they're supposed to know something that nobody actually taught them. Specifically, it's for:

College students and recent graduates who are navigating independence for the first time and discovering that "adulting" involves a lot more than they bargained for. If you've ever stood in a bank feeling confused, stared at a rental agreement wondering what half the terms mean, or called your parents to ask how to do laundry properly, this book is for you.

Young people who want to get it right the first time instead of learning through expensive mistakes. Maybe you've heard horror stories about friends who destroyed their credit scores, lost deposits on rental properties, or ended up in debt because they didn't understand how overdrafts work. You want to avoid those pitfalls and build good habits from the start.

Anyone who feels embarrassed about the basic stuff they don't know. There's no shame in not knowing how to negotiate with a landlord or what questions to ask when viewing a flat. The shame comes from pretending you know when you don't, then making decisions based on guesswork.

You don't need to be completely clueless to benefit from this book.

WHY THIS BOOK IS DIFFERENT

Most "adulting" advice falls into two unhelpful categories: either it's so basic it's insulting ("remember to eat vegetables!") or so advanced it assumes knowledge you don't have ("optimize your investment portfolio!"). This book lives in the practical middle ground where most of us actually need help.

Real-world scripts and templates: Instead of vague advice like "communicate professionally," you'll get actual email templates for common situations: how to report a maintenance issue to your landlord, how to ask your bank about a confusing charge, how to negotiate with roommates about bills.

Honest about what you don't need to know: There's a lot of adult advice that's technically correct but practically useless for most young people. This book focuses on skills you'll actually use in the next few years, not comprehensive guides to subjects you can learn later when they become relevant.

Written by someone who remembers being confused: This isn't advice from someone who's forgotten what it's like to be overwhelmed by basic tasks. The tone is more "older sibling who's figured some stuff out" than "parent lecturing about responsibility."

Designed for how you actually live: The advice accounts for student budgets, shared housing, digital communication, and modern banking.

It's not your parents' guide to adulting – it's yours.

WHAT'S COMING NEXT

This book is organized as a journey from the most urgent skills (managing money, securing housing) to the ones that build over time (career planning, long-term thinking). You don't need to read it in order, but each section builds on practical knowledge from earlier chapters.

We'll start with money basics – understanding bank accounts, building your first budget, and avoiding the credit mistakes that can follow you for years. Then we'll tackle housing and leases, demystifying the process of finding and keeping a place to live. From there, we'll cover daily life skills like cooking and cleaning, life administration like professional communication and time management, personal safety both online and offline, and finally work and future planning.

Throughout each section, you'll find real examples, common mistakes to avoid, and reassurance that everyone is figuring this out as they go along.

The goal is progress, not perfection.

Here's what I want you to know before you dive in: you're not behind, you're not stupid, and you're definitely not the only one who feels like everyone else got a manual that you missed. The embarrassment you feel about not knowing "basic" adult skills is completely normal and completely fixable.

Every competent adult you know had a moment (or several moments) of standing in a bank lobby feeling confused, or calling someone for help with something that seemed like it should be obvious. The difference between people who seem to have their act together and people who feel constantly overwhelmed isn't intelligence or natural ability – it's just information and practice.

The information is in this book. The practice starts now.

Stop apologizing for what you don't know and start building the skills that will serve you for life. You don't need to transform overnight. You just need to start where you are, with what you have, and learn one practical skill at a time.

Turn the page, pick a chapter that addresses your most pressing concern, and begin building the confident, capable adult you're already becoming.

1

Bank Accounts, Cards, and Not Getting Ripped Off

YOUR MONEY'S PERFECT HOME DECODED

Walking into a bank as a college student can feel like landing in a foreign country where everyone speaks fluent Acronym. APY, overdraft protection, minimum balance requirements... and you are just trying to figure out where your money actually goes.

Here is the part the bank ads do not shout about: basic accounts are much simpler than they look. If you get this foundation right, you can dodge hundreds of dollars in random fees over the next few years.

Picture it this way. Your checking account is your daily wallet. Your savings account is your digital piggy bank. Checking is where the action happens: groceries, rent, DoorDash, Venmo, ATM withdrawals. Savings is where you park money you do not want to touch right now and would like to grow by at least a tiny bit of interest while it waits.

Most students only need two accounts to cover almost everything: one checking account for regular spending and one savings account for emergencies and goals. That simple setup is enough for about 90% of student money situations without getting fancy, confusing, or expensive.

THE CHECKING ACCOUNT ESSENTIALS

A standard checking account usually comes with a debit card, a mobile app, and sometimes an old-school checkbook that will live in a drawer until graduation. This is your workhorse account. Your paychecks from campus jobs land here. Your rent, streaming subscriptions, and late-night pizza orders leave from here.

When you are choosing a checking account, a few details matter more than the color of the debit card. Look for accounts that do not charge a monthly maintenance fee, or at least give you easy ways to dodge it with direct deposits or a small minimum balance. Check that you can use plenty of ATMs without paying extra withdrawal fees. Make sure the mobile app is easy to use and does not crash every time you open it. Ask what happens if you spend more than you have and how much they charge for overdrafts.

Many banks and credit unions offer student checking accounts with friendlier rules than regular ones. These often waive monthly fees while you are in school, give you a little grace on overdrafts, or lower minimum balance requirements. The point is not to collect every perk possible; it is to choose an account that does not quietly drain your cash with fine print.

THE SAVINGS ACCOUNT REALITY

Savings accounts sound exciting because they earn interest. In reality, for most students we are talking “cents, not dollars.” Over time that interest will matter more, but right now the real power of a savings account is not the rate. It is the distance it puts between you and your money.

Most basic savings accounts limit how often you can pull money out each month. They sit slightly out of reach compared with checking, and that tiny bit of friction is exactly what helps. Money that is not one tap away from your Starbucks app is money you are more likely to still have when you actually need it.

Jacob opened his first bank account the week before starting college. His mom told him he needed both checking and savings. He did not see the point. Why not just keep everything in one place? Three months later, he understood. He had saved up for textbooks but left the money sitting in checking. One big night out plus a few impulse buys later, he logged in and realised his book money had turned into bar tabs.

The next morning he moved $200 into savings, labelled it "textbooks and emergencies," and left it alone. With that money parked somewhere slightly harder to access, he stopped "accidentally" spending it. The balance in checking felt like real spending money again, not a mysterious pile that included rent, books, and panic funds.

SETTING UP SUCCESS

When you open your accounts, use the chance to ask questions. Ask about student discounts, how their overdraft system works, whether they have overdraft grace for small transactions, and what kinds of alerts you can turn on in the app. Bank employees talk to confused new customers every day; saying "this is my first account and I want to avoid fees" is completely normal.

The structure you build here connects directly to everything in the next chapter about budgeting. A clean setup—one main checking account and one savings account—makes tracking your money so much easier than trying to juggle three random apps and a half-remembered Venmo balance.

DEBIT OR CREDIT CARDS DECODED

The plastic rectangles in your wallet might look like twins, but debit and credit cards behave very differently. Understanding that difference will save you from awkward declined payments, surprise fees, and expensive mistakes all the way through college and beyond.

A debit card pulls money directly from your checking account. If you do not have enough in there, the payment should fail unless your bank lets it go through and charges you an overdraft fee. A credit card lets you borrow up to a certain limit from the bank and pay it back later. With debit, you are spending your own money. With credit, you are spending the bank's money and promising to pay them back.

That simple distinction changes everything from how fraud is handled to whether you can book certain services.

WHY MOST STUDENTS START WITH DEBIT

Debit cards feel safer when you are just starting out because they come with a built-in speed limit. You can only spend what is in your checking account before the card starts getting declined or fees kick in. For a lot of students building their first budget, that natural boundary helps stop small mistakes from turning into big debt.

Your debit card is tied straight to that checking account you set up earlier. Use it at the campus bookstore, and the money leaves your account almost immediately. Open your app, and you will see the purchase sitting in your recent transactions within a few hours. That instant feedback makes it easier to see how each swipe changes your balance.

THE CREDIT CARD ADVANTAGE

Credit cards add an extra layer of responsibility but also come with real benefits once you know how to use them. One of the biggest is fraud protection. If someone steals your credit card info and goes on a shopping spree, it is the bank's money at risk first. You report the charges, the bank investigates, and you do not have to pay for the suspicious transactions while they sort it out.

With debit card fraud, the money disappears from your checking account right away. You can usually get it back if you report it quickly, but until then you might be scrambling to cover rent, food, or gas while the bank reviews your case.

Plenty of companies also prefer or require credit cards for deposits and holds. Hotels, car rental companies, and some online services like to put a temporary "hold" on a card in case of damage, late fees, or extra charges.

Jane discovered this during a weekend trip with friends. She had $300 in her checking account and only a debit card. The hotel wanted to put a $150 hold on her card for incidentals. That hold would have frozen half of her spending money for up to a week, leaving her with $150 for gas, food, and everything else. Her friend used a credit card instead. The hold sat on the card's available limit and did not touch her actual bank balance, so her cash for the trip stayed untouched.

THE OVERDRAFT TRAP

Even a debit card can cause trouble when overdrafts enter the picture. Imagine you have $20 in your account and buy something for $25. Some banks will approve the transaction anyway and then charge you a $35 overdraft fee. Suddenly that $25 purchase costs $60.

This becomes painful when several transactions go through while your account is below zero. A coffee here, a snack there, a couple of small rideshares… each can trigger its own fee. What felt like a $30 day turns into a $130 disaster when the fees hit.

Most banks give you the option to turn off overdraft coverage for everyday card purchases. In that case, if there is not enough money in your account, the payment just gets declined at the register. That can feel embarrassing in the moment, but in the long run, it is often much cheaper than paying fee after fee.

Knowing how your cards behave—and changing those settings if you need to—puts you in a much stronger position for the budgeting strategies coming up, where you will start tracking spending by account and card type.

DODGE THESE HIDDEN BANKING TRAPS

Banks make a lot of their money from fees people never planned on paying. College students are easy targets because they are new to banking, busy, and often working with very tight budgets where one mistake can snowball fast.

An overdraft happens when your account goes below zero and the bank still lets payments go through. Instead of rejecting the card, the bank "helps" by covering the difference and then charges you for the favor. Fees of $25 to $35 per transaction are common. That is how a $3 coffee turns into a $38 memory you do not want.

The worst part is how fast those fees stack up. Imagine you have $50 in your account. You buy a $3 coffee, an $8 lunch, and a $45 textbook, not realizing a bill is about to clear. If all three purchases push you into the negative, the bank can charge three separate overdraft fees. You spent $56 and walk away owing more than $100 in penalties.

Some student checking accounts offer special overdraft features like lower fees or small interest-free buffers. Regular accounts, though, usually pair overdraft fees with interest on the negative balance. After graduation, any student perks often disappear, so it is better to treat overdrafts as emergency-only, not as "extra money" you can lean on.

Then there are the smaller "gotcha" fees. Monthly maintenance fees for not keeping a high enough balance. ATM fees when you use another bank's machine. That $2.50 fee might not sound like much, but if you hit out-of-network ATMs twice a week, that is about $260 a year just to see your own money.

International transaction fees add another leak. Any time you shop from a non-US website or use your card abroad, your bank may tack on an extra 2 to 3 per cent. During a study abroad semester or a big trip, those small percentages quietly inflate the cost of every meal, ticket, and souvenir.

Overdraft "protection" deserves extra side-eye. The name makes it sound like a safety feature, but what it often protects is the bank's ability to charge you. With this setting on, your card keeps working even when your balance does not, and every covered transaction can generate a fee.

You can usually tell your bank you would rather have the transaction declined instead. Yes, a declined card at checkout is awkward. But that two-second cringe is often better than a three-figure fee total waiting for you in your app the next morning.

Alexander thought he was on top of things. Before going out, he checked his balance and saw $47 available. What he forgot was the $45 gym membership set to auto-pay the next morning. He spent $52 that night on bus fares, drinks, and late-night food. Each purchase nudged his account further negative, and each one carried a $30 overdraft fee. What should have been a $52 night turned into $172 once the fees landed. After that, he set an informal rule to keep at least $100 in his account and turned on low-balance alerts in his app.

A couple of simple protections go a long way. Many banking apps let you set alerts when your balance drops below a number you choose, like $100. That text is your "slow down" sign before fees start hitting. Some banks also let you connect your savings account to your checking account so that if you do go negative, the bank automatically pulls money from savings instead of charging an overdraft fee. There may still be a small transfer charge, but it is usually much cheaper than multiple overdrafts.

All of this plugs directly into the budgeting chapter coming up, where you will start tracking what leaves your accounts and why. It is much easier to build a plan when your bank is not quietly charging you every time you breathe near a card reader.

SHIELD YOUR MONEY FROM DIGITAL THIEVES

Scammers love college students. You are new to banking, juggling classes, jobs, and a social life, and you might not have seen all the tricks yet. A convincing email or text can empty an account in hours if you are stressed, distracted, and just trying to get through your to-do list.

Real banks have certain rules they follow, and learning those rules is one of the easiest ways to protect yourself. A legitimate bank will not ask for your full password, PIN, or entire card number in a text, email, or out-of-the-blue phone call. They already have those details. Anyone who asks you to read them out or type them into a link they just sent should set off alarm bells.

When banks contact you for real, they usually mention information they already know, like the last four digits of your account or a recent transaction amount. They tell you to log in through the official app or main website, not through a random link.

Scam messages often lean hard on urgency. They say things like "Your account will be locked in 24 hours" or "Suspicious activity detected—click now." They want you to panic, tap the link, and enter your details before you have time to think.

Web addresses are another clue. Scammers buy domains that look almost right: "chase-secure-login.com" instead of "chase.com," "bofa-support-help.com" instead of the real Bank of America site. On a phone screen those fake addresses can be easy to miss, especially if you are in a hurry. The pages they lead to often look exactly like real bank logins, but every detail you type there goes straight to the scammer.

Legitimate messages from your bank will address you by name, reference an account you actually have, and give you a way to check what is going on through official channels. If anything feels even slightly off, step away from the message. Open your banking app yourself or type your bank's web address into your browser.

Never call a phone number that appears in a suspicious text or email. Those numbers often send you straight to more scammers pretending to be "fraud departments." Use the number on the back of your card or on the bank's official site instead.

Mary got a text that looked exactly like previous messages from her bank. Same logo, same tone, same style. It warned about "suspicious activity" and told her to click a link to secure her account. The web address included her bank's name with an extra word tacked on. She remembered her older brother's advice: never tap a link in a banking text. She ignored it, opened the official app instead, and saw no odd transactions. Then she called the number on the back of her card. The bank confirmed that the text was fake and that similar messages had gone out to thousands of people. If she had logged in through that link, scammers could have drained her account within hours.

A few habits can keep you ahead of most fraud attempts. Turn on two-factor authentication in your banking apps so a password alone is not enough to get in. Use fingerprint or face recognition login if your phone supports it. Check your account regularly—every few days, not once a month. If you see a transaction you do not recognise, contact your bank immediately through the app or official number.

These security habits will become part of your normal routine once you start budgeting in the next chapter. You will be looking at your accounts more often anyway, so you will naturally get better at spotting the difference between "I totally bought that" and "I have no idea what that charge is." And that awareness is one of the strongest shields your money can have.

2

Budgeting When You've Never Had to Before

MONEY SOURCES THAT FUND YOUR FUTURE

Before any budget can work, you need to know one thing first: what money is actually coming in and when.

Student income is chaos in a hoodie. It shows up in bursts, from different places, on random days. Compared to a regular monthly paycheck, college money is like getting fed in surprise tapas.

Most working adults get a steady paycheck on the same two Fridays each month. They can map out rent, bills, groceries, done. As a student, your money arrives in weird chunks throughout the year, which creates problems your parents probably did *not* deal with when they were swiping their student IDs.

Let's untangle it.

THE BIG THREE INCOME SOURCES

For most students, money shows up from three main places: student loans and grants, part-time work, and family support. Each behaves very differently, which is why treating them all "like a paycheck" usually backfires.

Student loans and grants usually hit your account in a few big drops each academic year, not as neat monthly deposits. Depending on your school's system, that might mean money arriving at the start of fall semester, the start of spring, and sometimes at the beginning of summer classes. The amount depends on your family's income, your school, and whether you are full-time or part-time.

The classic mistake? Spending like that first big lump is your *monthly* income instead of money that has to last for months.

Part-time work is a different rhythm. Money from weekend shifts, campus jobs, tutoring, babysitting, or summer work depends on your hours and the season. Retail or food service might give you tons of shifts around holidays, then vanish during finals when your boss assumes you are drowning in exams (spoiler: you are).

Family support adds another layer. Some parents send a set amount every month. Others swoop in with Venmo when your "I am broke and eating ramen" texts start appearing. You might get help for specific things, like textbooks, car repairs, or housing deposits. Some families are steady. Others are more "call us if it is an emergency."

REAL STUDENT MONEY PATTERNS

Adrian felt rich when his $3,000 loan hit his account in August. For the first time in his life, there were four digits sitting in his name. By November, he was staring at $200 and trying not to panic. The next loan disbursement was months away.

The problem was not that the loan was too small. The problem was that he had been spending like he made $1,000 every month instead of remembering that $3,000 had to stretch across the whole semester. His weekend job at a local bar brought in about $300 a month, but only while school was in session. Over winter break, his shifts vanished. His spending did not.

Isabella's issue looked different on paper but felt just as stressful. Her parents promised to send $200 a month for living expenses. On a spreadsheet, that sounded simple. In real life, the money arrived whenever life allowed—sometimes a week early, sometimes two weeks late.

After a couple of close calls with rent and grocery runs, she learned to keep a buffer in her checking account (from Chapter 1) because she could not reliably predict when the "monthly" transfer would land. The support was real; the timing was chaos.

TRACKING YOUR INCOME REALITY

The goal here is not to make your money perfect. It is to make it visible.

Start by listing every way cash enters your life. Write down the guaranteed money first: student loans, confirmed grants, scholarships that renew automatically. Then add the income you can *probably* count on most months, like regular part-time job wages. Finally, note the "maybe" money—family help, odd jobs, extra shifts that pop up during holidays, side hustles that come and go.

Next to each one, write down:

- roughly *when* it usually shows up
- how much you can realistically expect, not your fantasy version

This simple map becomes the foundation for the rest of the chapter. It explains why you feel loaded in September and panicked in January. It also shows where your income might randomly disappear at the exact moment your bills do not.

Learning this now saves you from the "I have no money and my payment just bounced" spiral. That matters for your stress levels *and* for your future credit score in Chapter 3, where missed payments and overdrafts do not just hurt today—they follow you.

YOUR MONEY'S TWO PERSONALITIES EXPLAINED

Once you know what is coming in, the next step is seeing where it has to go versus where you get to choose.

This is where fixed and flexible expenses come in. It is like finally getting the rulebook for a game you have been playing blind. Fixed expenses are the non-negotiables that stay close to the same every month. Flexible expenses are where your decisions and moods show up.

Understanding the difference is a cheat code for adult life.

FIXED EXPENSES: THE UNMOVABLES

Fixed expenses are the bills that show up whether you are ready or not. They are your financial bedrock: rent, your phone plan, insurance payments, subscriptions you have committed to, minimum loan payments, that gym membership you *swear* you will start using next week.

Once you sign for a 12-month lease or lock into a phone contract, backing out usually costs you more than sticking with it. This is why the contracts stuff from Chapter 1 matters more than it looks at first glance. Fixed expenses are slow to change and often involve cancellation fees, notice periods, or awkward phone calls.

You cannot tweak these easily in the middle of the month. They just… happen. Which is exactly why they need to be counted first.

FLEXIBLE EXPENSES: YOUR CONTROL ZONE

Flexible expenses are your daily decision playground. Food, groceries, nights out, rideshares, clothes, random Target runs, coffee, takeout, makeup, "I just needed a little treat" purchases—this is where your personality spills all over your bank statement.

They change based on your mood, your stress level, your social life, and how many "let's just grab food after class" invites you say yes to.

When money gets tight, this is the category you can actually move. You may not be able to email your landlord and ask to "vibe your rent down this month," but you *can* swap one takeout night for pasta at home or skip that one impulse purchase that is cute but not crucial.

SEMI-FIXED: THE MIDDLE GROUND

Some bills live in a grey zone between fixed and flexible. You need them, but your choices change the amount.

Think utilities if you live off campus—electricity, gas, water. You cannot cancel them, but you do control how high the heat is, how long your showers are, and whether your lights are on all night for no reason.

These costs do not disappear, but they are not as stubborn as rent either.

REAL STUDENT REALITY CHECK

Olivia could not work out why her bank account kept hitting zero before the end of the month. On paper, her student loan gave her about $1,000 a month to work with. That sounded decent.

When she finally wrote everything down, the picture got clearer. Her fixed expenses were $400 for rent, $25 for her phone plan, $10 for Spotify, and $20 for a gym membership she barely used. Together, those came to $455 every month.

That meant almost half of her "$1,000 budget" was already locked up before she had eaten a single meal or taken a bus anywhere. Suddenly it made sense why her flexible spending on food, nights out, and random "treat yourself" shopping pushed her into overdraft.

She cancelled the gym membership, because watching Netflix did not require a treadmill. The rent and phone bill were staying, but now she could see clearly that the real number she controlled was around $545, not $1,000. That switch alone made her budget feel much less like a mystery and more like a plan.

WHY THIS MATTERS FOR YOUR FUTURE

Once you know what is fixed, semi-fixed, and flexible, every future money decision gets easier.

Thinking about upgrading your phone plan? You will instantly know that you are shrinking your future flexible money. Considering signing up for three different streaming services? You will see that you are quietly building a little army of fixed expenses that show up whether you watch them or not.

This awareness is gold when you hit Chapter 3 and start dealing with credit cards and your credit score. Lenders care about how well you juggle those regular commitments. Your future apartment, car, and even some jobs will care too.

BUDGET TEMPLATE THAT ACTUALLY WORKS

Most budgeting advice assumes you are a full-time grown-up with a regular monthly salary. You are not there yet. You get lump sums, weird timing, surprise help, and random gaps.

You need a system that can handle "loan in August, broke in October" without collapsing. Something simple enough that you will actually use it, not an over-designed spreadsheet you open twice and abandon.

Forget the budgeting apps with 47 categories and pie charts that look like modern art. You need a structure that still makes sense when your loan arrived three months ago and you are trying to make the last $200 stretch.

THE THREE-COLUMN SYSTEM

A good starting point is a three-column setup you can draw on paper, in your notes app, or in a basic spreadsheet. Label the columns money in, must pay, and everything else.

Under money in, list each income source and roughly when it arrives. That means your student loans, grants, regular job income, and typical family support. Use realistic numbers, not best-case fantasies.

Under must pay, list your fixed expenses from earlier: rent, phone plan, minimum loan payments, essential insurance, and a basic food number you absolutely need to survive. This is the boring but necessary column.

What is left after that becomes everything else. That chunk is your flexible spending, emergency cushion, and savings. It is also your guilt-free money, because you know the essentials are covered.

WEEKLY THINKING WINS

Student money rarely lines up neatly with "per month." Switching your brain to weekly amounts makes everything easier.

When a loan or big payment drops into your checking account (from Chapter 1), take the total and divide it by the number of weeks until the next big payment will arrive. That answer is your weekly budget from that source.

Then add your weekly job income on top. Suddenly, your money has a rhythm. You are no longer guessing, you are working with a real number. This is how you kill off the classic feast-then-famine cycle where September is sushi and Ubers, and November is instant noodles and tears.

BUILD YOUR BUFFER ZONE

Some budgeting advice tells you to give every single dollar a specific job. That is cute in theory. Then your laptop dies the week before finals, your car battery quits, or you need emergency travel money to get home.

Student life is unpredictable. You will have surprise expenses that do not care what your spreadsheet says.

So instead of building a "perfect" budget that collapses the second life happens, build in a buffer—some money that is not assigned to anything yet. That cushion turns "oh no, this ruins everything" into "annoying, but I can handle it."

REAL STUDENT SUCCESS STORY

Marcus downloaded three different budgeting apps before admitting he hated all of them. They were too busy, too detailed, and too easy to ignore.

He ended up with a simple weekly system on paper. First, he added up all his income for the semester. His $3,000 loan spread over 12 weeks meant $250 per week. Then he calculated his fixed weekly costs—rent, phone, bus pass, and a realistic food minimum—which worked out to about $115 a week. That left $135 of true spending money each week for fun, extras, and emergencies.

Any extra cash from part-time work became bonus money. Some weeks, he used it for bigger things like concert tickets or trips. Other weeks, he let it roll into his buffer.

The system worked not because it was fancy, but because he could explain it without opening an app. It was simple enough to stick with, flexible enough to survive surprise costs, and clear enough that he always knew whether he could say yes to plans.

YOUR SIMPLE TEMPLATE

You can build your own version in about five minutes. Start with three lines and fill them out based on your numbers:

Weekly income: $____

Weekly fixed costs: $____

Weekly flexible money: $____

Update it when something big changes, like a new job or a new lease. Do not obsess over making every decimal perfect. The point is to know roughly where you stand, not to impress your calculator.

This one little template sets you up for the decisions in Chapter 3, where good budgeting habits translate directly into stronger credit and better options.

WHEN FIVE DOLLARS BECOMES FIFTY

Small purchases are sneaky. A $5 snack or coffee barely registers in your brain. It feels like nothing. The problem is that your budget does not care how *small* something feels; it only cares how often you do it.

Twenty $5 "it's no big deal" moments are a very big deal. That is $100.

Your brain tends to treat one big $50 purchase as Important and ten $5 ones as "basically free." So you agonize over whether to spend $50 on a textbook, while casually spending the same $50 across random snacks, little treats, and delivery fees without even noticing.

THE REAL COST REVELATION

Try this experiment once, and you will never unsee the results.

For one normal week, write down every single purchase under $10. Coffee, vending machines, late-night fries, campus shop runs, random bus rides when you *could* have walked—everything. Put each one in your notes app the second you buy it so nothing gets "forgotten."

Most people are shocked by the total at the end. All those "tiny" buys form an amount that could have covered several days of groceries or a serious chunk of your rent.

WEEKLY MENTAL MATH

Get into the habit of flipping daily habits into weekly and monthly numbers. A $5 coffee every day? That is $35 a week, roughly $140 a month. Suddenly it is not "just coffee," it is a bill that costs more than many phone plans.

The same trick works for subscriptions. That $9.99 streaming service you forgot about? It is quietly chewing up around $2.50 of your weekly flexible money from your budget template. One or two of those is fine. Five of them is a problem.

SMART SPENDING BARRIERS

You do not have to turn into a monk to get your money under control. You just need a few speed bumps between "I want it" and "I bought it."

One option is to leave your main card at home for non-essential trips and bring a set amount of cash instead. Physically handing over bills feels a lot more real than tapping your phone. Another is to keep your card somewhere you have to unzip, reach for, or stand up to grab. Those extra seconds give your brain time to ask, "Do I actually care about this, or am I just bored?"

These little barriers are not about punishment. They are about making sure you spend on purpose, not by default.

STUDENT REALITY CHECK

Emily was constantly confused about where her money went. Her big bills were paid, but her account still felt empty too often.

So she tracked every purchase under $10 for one week. By Sunday, the list looked something like this: meal deals at $3 five times, coffee at $2.50 four times, snacks between classes at $1.50 six times, and a few random campus shop buys at $4 three times.

When she added it all up, it came to $41 in one week. That is about $164 a month on things she barely remembered buying.

She did not quit everything at once. She kept her Tuesday coffee tradition with friends because it made her week better. On other days, she made coffee in her dorm. The point was not to eliminate joy; it was to make sure she was actually choosing it.

YOUR MONEY AWARENESS WEEK

Pick one ordinary week—not a special "I am trying to be good" week—and track every small purchase. Do not change anything yet. Just write down what you spend and how much, the moment you spend it.

At the end of the week, total it up and multiply by four to see what that pattern looks like over a month. Then compare that number to your weekly and monthly flexible money from your simple template.

Suddenly, your daily decisions and your overall budget stop feeling like two separate worlds. You will see exactly how those tiny taps and swipes add up—and that awareness is the first step to making your money behave.

3

Credit Scores & Cards - Future You Will Thank You

YOUR CREDIT SCORE SHAPES TOMORROW

Picture this: you are 25, finally ready to move out of roommate chaos and into your own place. You find an apartment you love, you have the security deposit saved, and your budget from Chapter 2 says, "Yep, you can afford this."

Then the landlord runs a credit check and comes back with, "Sorry, your application was denied."

You did not do anything *wrong*... you just do not exist on paper yet. No credit history does not register as "blank." It registers as "risky."

A credit score is a three-digit number, usually somewhere between 300 and 850, that tells lenders how you have handled borrowed money in the past. Think of it as your money GPA that follows you for years. Banks, landlords, credit card companies, cell phone carriers, and sometimes employers use it to decide if they trust you with their money, property, or services.

That one number shows up everywhere. It helps decide whether you get approved for apartments, car loans, or a future mortgage. It shapes what interest rate you pay on those loans. It can even influence how much you pay for car insurance or whether you have to put down a deposit just to turn the lights on in a new place. A strong score can save you thousands of dollars over your adult life. A weak one quietly makes everything more expensive.

Brandon ran into this wall right after graduation. He had a full-time job, savings in the bank, and a decent budget. On the outside, he looked responsible. On paper, he was a ghost. He had never used a credit card, never taken out a loan, and never had any bills in his name. The apartment complex he applied to required a minimum score. With no history, he did not meet it. He could only move in after his parents co-signed. That was the moment he realised "I avoid debt" is not the same as "I have good credit."

The numbers make the difference painfully obvious. Someone with excellent credit—say, a score of 750 or higher—might get a car loan at around 3 percent interest. Someone with a score under 600 might get stuck near 15 percent. On a $20,000 car loan over five years, that gap adds roughly $3,500 in extra interest. Same car, same road, completely different price tag.

WHAT ACTUALLY CREATES YOUR CREDIT SCORE

Credit scores are not magic; they come from a few specific ingredients that credit bureaus track over time.

The biggest chunk of your score comes from your payment history. Do you pay your bills on time, or do you miss due dates and pay late? Every on-time payment is a little thumbs-up. Every late payment is a little red flag.

Next is your credit utilisation, which is how much of your available credit you are using. If your total credit limit across all cards is $1,000 and you are carrying a $800 balance, that is 80 percent utilisation. Scoring models prefer to see this number much lower—ideally under about 30 percent.

The length of your credit history also matters. Lenders like seeing accounts that have been open and managed responsibly for several years. New credit lines and the average age of your accounts both factor into that.

Types of credit (credit mix) play a smaller role. Having only credit cards is fine as a student, but later on, having a mix of accounts like installment loans and cards can help. Finally, new credit inquiries—those "hard pulls" that happen when you apply for a new card or loan—make up the last piece. Too many in a short time can drag your score down temporarily.

Here is what blindsides most college students: this whole system moves slowly. You cannot wake up one morning, decide "I need a great score," and have one by next week. It takes months and often years of small, boring, on-time payments to build a solid record.

That checking account you opened in Chapter 1? Great for daily money management. Useless for your credit score. Bank accounts and debit cards usually do not show up on your credit report. The credit card we are about to talk about *does*.

Starting early is a favor to future you—the one who wants to get an apartment without dragging a parent into every application.

STUDENT CREDIT BUILDING MADE SIMPLE

The good news is you do not need a huge income or a finance degree to build credit. You just need a strategy and some patience.

Building credit is basically a long-running trust exercise. You borrow small amounts, pay them back reliably, and repeat. Over time, your score starts saying, "This person follows through."

The rule that runs underneath everything: never borrow more than you can comfortably pay back from your existing budget. You are not trying to impress anyone by using credit. You are using it as training wheels for your financial future.

Students usually start in a few common ways. Some get a student credit card with a low limit—maybe $300 or $500—designed for people new to credit. Others become authorised users on a parent's card, which means the account shows up on their credit report even if they never physically use the card. The key in both cases is using credit for small, regular purchases you would have made anyway and then paying those off in full.

Grace began building credit in her sophomore year with a student card that had a $500 limit. She only used it for her music streaming subscription and groceries. Then she set up automatic payments from her checking account (from Chapter 1) so the full balance cleared every month.

She did this quietly in the background for two years. By the time her friends were getting turned down for phone contracts and credit cards, she had a solid score. That record helped her qualify for a good rate on a student loan and sign a lease on an apartment without a co-signer.

GOLDEN RULES OF STUDENT CREDIT BUILDING

A few simple habits will make or break your score.

The first one: do not carry a balance on purpose. If you cannot pay for something in cash today, do not put it on a credit card. Cards are tools for building a track record, not a way to pretend you make more than you do. Paying the balance in full every month keeps you away from interest charges and tells lenders you are reliable.

The second: keep your utilisation low. Even if your limit is $500 and you *could* pay off a $480 balance, running your card that high all the time is not ideal. Try to stay under about 30 percent of your limit most of the time. On a $500 card, that means aiming to keep your balance under roughly $150.

The third: never miss a payment. Set up autopay, reminders, calendar alerts—whatever it takes. One late payment can stick to your credit report for years and undo months of careful work.

There are also some clear don'ts. Applying for several credit cards at once triggers multiple hard inquiries, which can temporarily lower your score and make you look desperate for credit. Closing your very first card just because you got a "better" one can shorten your average account age and actually hurt your score; it is often smarter to keep that first card open with a tiny recurring charge. And lending your card to friends is a shortcut to disaster. You are legally responsible for every charge, even if they promise to pay you back.

The payoff for following these rules shows up when you start apartment hunting, buying a car, or signing up for utilities. Landlords and companies like dealing with people who have a track record of paying on time. Good credit does not just open doors, it sometimes gets you in without extra deposits or co-signers.

SMART CREDIT CARD MOVES THAT PROTECT YOUR WALLET

Credit cards are like power tools. In the right hands, they make everything easier. In the wrong hands, they punch holes in everything. The difference often comes down to one rule: never spend money you do not already have.

Used well, credit cards are just a convenient way to pay for things you already budgeted for, with bonus fraud protection and credit-building points attached. Your mental script should be "I'll put this on the card now and pay it off from my checking account," not "I'll figure it out later."

A few guardrails help a lot. Paying the full statement balance every month keeps you out of interest and tells your credit report, "This person follows through." Keeping your utilisation under about 30 percent keeps your score happier. Turning on automatic payments and alerts means you do not get ambushed by due dates or weird charges you forgot were pending.

Nathan learned the hard way what happens when you ignore those guardrails. He put an $800 spring break trip on his credit card because "I'll never get this chance again." The minimum payments looked small, so he assumed it would be easy. Months later, the balance had barely moved because those minimums mostly covered interest. By the time he finally cleared the card, the $800 trip had cost him more than $1,200. The memories were fun; the two years of extra stress were not.

The better way to use a card is boring—and that is exactly why it works. Pick a few regular expenses you already have in your budget—groceries, gas, or a streaming service—and run them through your credit card. Then either pay them off right away from your checking account or let autopay clear the full balance at the end of the month. Your actual spending does not change; your credit report just gets a polished highlight reel.

Choosing the right card helps too. Student cards that offer small cashback on groceries or have no foreign transaction fees for study abroad can be genuinely useful. Fancy travel reward cards with high annual fees make less sense if your spending is mostly coffee, textbooks, and takeout. Rewards are only "rewards" if they fit how you already live.

Track your spending more closely than you think you need to. Because no physical cash leaves your hand, it is easy for card purchases to blur together. Check your card balance at least once a week and compare it against your budget categories from Chapter 2. Most banking apps now group transactions for you into things like "food," "transportation," and "shopping," which makes it easier to see when one area is getting out of control.

There are a couple of bright red flags to watch for. If you are only making the minimum payment because the full amount feels scary, your budget needs a reset. If you are using credit to cover basics like groceries and bills because you do not have enough income, that is a sign of an income problem, not a sign that you should open another card. Credit should support your plan, not hide the gap between your plan and reality.

Once you have these fundamentals down, you will be in a much better position when we hit Chapter 4 and talk about housing. Strong credit and calm money habits give you more choices —dorms, shared apartments, off-campus rentals—and a better shot at hearing "you're approved" instead of "you will need a co-signer."

FINANCIAL TRAPS THAT DRAIN YOUR WALLET

Of course, not every financial product is on your side. Some companies design their offers specifically for people who are stressed, impatient, or new to money. The pitch sounds friendly. The fine print is a trap.

Payday loans are a classic example. They promise quick cash "until your next paycheck," but the interest rates can be 400 percent or higher when you do the math over a year. Missing one payment can start a cycle of borrowing just to pay off what you borrowed before.

Buy now, pay later services operate more quietly. Splitting a purchase into "just $25 a month" sounds easy. It stays easy when there is only one plan. The problem starts when you have eight of those plans running at once for clothes, tech, textbooks, and takeout. Suddenly, "just $25" has turned into hundreds of dollars in monthly instalments you barely remember agreeing to.

Some credit cards are built the same way, with high annual fees, huge penalty interest rates after a single late payment, and terms that make it hard to ever reach a zero balance.

Helen slid into this in her first year. She started using Klarna and Afterpay for clothes, books, and food, telling herself it was "only $20 a month" here and there. After a semester, she added everything up and realised she now had over $200 in monthly payments across different platforms. Then she missed one. Fees hit. Her credit score dipped at the exact time she was trying to build it. She eventually paid everything off and made herself a rule: if she could not pay for something up front, she would not sign up for a plan that pretended she could.

The pattern behind all these traps is the same. They focus your attention on how *little* you pay today, not on the total cost or how long the payments last. They look like help, but they make their profit from your stress and your impatience.

A safer approach is to treat any "super convenient" finance offer with suspicion. Pause before saying yes. Ask what the total cost will be, how long you will be paying, and what happens if you are late. Compare that to your weekly budget from Chapter 2. If the answers make your stomach tighten, your finances probably will not enjoy it either.

TURNING THIS INTO ACTION

You do not have to overhaul your entire life tonight. A few small moves start the credit-building snowball.

Check whether you qualify for a basic student credit card with a low limit, or talk to a financially responsible family member about being added as an authorised user on their card. Once you have access to some form of credit, turn on automatic full-balance payments and alerts for upcoming due dates.

Then choose one regular expense—maybe a streaming subscription or your weekly gas and grocery run—and put that on your card. Each month, pay it off from your checking account. You are not spending more. You are just giving the credit system a chance to notice that you exist and that you are consistent.

As your score grows, more options will quietly open up: better loan rates, easier approvals, fewer deposits. And when we move into the housing chapter next, you will be glad you started building that money GPA before you ever stepped into an apartment viewing.

4

Dorms, Flatshares, and First Rentals Explained

YOUR HOUSING OPTIONS DECODED

Housing is where your budget and your real life collide. The place you choose affects how much you spend, how much you sleep, how much you study, and how easy it is to have an actual social life instead of just waving at people on Zoom.

After getting your money and credit foundations set up in Chapter 3, you are ready for one of the biggest line items in your budget: where you live. Rent will likely be your largest expense, so it is worth actually understanding the options instead of just grabbing the first listing that looks cute on Instagram.

UNIVERSITY RESIDENCE HALLS

Dorms are the classic first-year move for a reason. They usually bundle a lot together: housing, utilities, internet, and often a meal plan, all rolled into one predictable bill. That means no surprise electric bill in January because your roommate believes in "tropical climate" as a lifestyle.

You pay for that convenience, though. On a cost-per-square-foot basis, dorms are usually more expensive than living off-campus. You also trade some independence for structure. Residence halls have rules about guests, noise, quiet hours, and sometimes even what appliances you are allowed to bring.

But the built-in social life is massive.

There are people everywhere. Floor events, RA programs, movie nights, game rooms, study lounges—dorms are designed so you can meet people without ever leaving the building. When you are brand new to campus and still figuring out where the dining hall is, that ready-made community right outside your door is a huge support system.

SHARED HOUSES OR APARTMENTS

After the first year, a lot of students move into shared off-campus housing: renting a house or apartment with roommates. The big draw is cost and freedom. Splitting rent and utilities can be cheaper per person, and you can choose your roommates, decorate how you want, and feel more like a regular adult.

The trade-off? You now run the household.

You (collectively) are responsible for paying rent on time, setting up and paying utilities, choosing an internet plan, taking out the trash, and figuring out why the Wi-Fi dies every time it rains. Those budgeting skills from Chapter 2 suddenly become very real when the power company does not care whose turn it was to pay the bill.

The social vibe shifts too. Instead of an entire building full of students, your day-to-day world is your roommates and whoever drops by. That can be amazing if you chose well, or very intense if you did not.

Then there is the "solo apartment" dream. A studio or one-bedroom gives you total control of your space: your mess, your playlist, your thermostat. It is also almost always the most expensive option.

Frederick thought he wanted total independence, so he rented a studio for his second year. Within two months he realised he was paying nearly twice as much as his friends in shared houses and felt weirdly lonely. No roommate jokes in the kitchen, no "you up?" from the next room during exam week—just him, his plants, and a very high rent.

Katherine took a different path. She stayed in the dorms her first year to ease into college life and take advantage of the social side. By second year, she felt ready for more independence and wanted to save money, so she moved into a house with three friends. The step-by-step approach gave her both: support when she needed it and freedom when she was ready for it.

Next, we are going to get into the unglamorous but crucial stuff: leases, deposits, and how not to accidentally sign your life away.

BEYOND THE PRICE TAG ESSENTIALS

The cheapest rent on paper is not always the cheapest life in reality. A "bargain" apartment that destroys your commute, wrecks your sleep, and eats your money in hidden costs is not actually a bargain.

Now that you have a rough sense of the main housing types, it is time to look past the number on the listing and think like Future You.

LOCATION CONSIDERATIONS

How close you live to campus changes your entire daily rhythm. Being able to walk or bike to class saves money and time and makes it easier to say yes to last-minute "come study with us" or "we're getting food after lab" plans.

If you live farther out, public transportation becomes a key character in your life. Check how often buses actually run, especially at night and on weekends. A place that looks great on Google Maps but leaves you stranded after 7 p.m. will get very annoying, very fast.

Nearby basics matter more than you think: grocery stores, laundromats (if you do not have in-unit laundry), pharmacies, and somewhere you can grab food when you forget to eat all day. The less you have to trek across town for basic errands, the more time and money you save.

Safety is non-negotiable. Visit the neighborhood during the day and after dark if you can. How does it feel? Are there people around? Is it well-lit? Your peace of mind is worth more than shaving $30 off the rent.

HIDDEN COSTS THAT CAN BLOW YOUR BUDGET

Rent is only the headline. The fine print lives in utilities and extras.

If utilities are not included, you will be paying for electricity, gas or heat, water, and trash—sometimes through separate companies. Older buildings with bad insulation can cost a lot more to keep warm or cool. Newer places might be more efficient but come with higher base rent.

Internet is another wild card. Some rentals include Wi-Fi, others expect you to set it up yourself. Plans and speeds vary a lot, and "cheap but useless" is not a great deal when you are trying to stream lectures and submit assignments.

Then there are transport costs. Living 45 minutes away might cut your rent, but if that means a monthly bus pass, occasional Lyft rides when you miss the last bus, and extra trips back and forth, the total can easily beat the "more expensive" place closer in.

You might also need renters' insurance. It is an extra monthly cost, but it protects your stuff if anything goes wrong—leaks, theft, or that one roommate who forgets there is literally a stove on. Sometimes, your parents' homeowner's insurance will cover your belongings while you are at college; sometimes it will not. It is worth one phone call to find out.

QUALITY OF LIFE FACTORS

Some things do not show up on the listing, but they decide whether you actually *like* living somewhere.

Natural light plays a big role in your mood and energy. A space with one tiny window that faces a brick wall might look fine in staged photos and feel depressing in real life.

Noise matters too. Living directly above a bar might sound fun until you are trying to sleep before an 8 a.m. exam. Busy roads, train lines, thin walls, upstairs stompers—these all change how restful a place feels.

Kitchen space, storage, and bathroom sharing are the daily details that either make life smooth or drive you up the wall. Four people and one bathroom is very different from two people and two bathrooms. So is "one tiny fridge for six roommates" versus enough space that someone's leftovers are not always being sacrificed.

Hannah found what looked like a dream deal: a room $50 cheaper per month than anywhere else on her list. It looked great in the photos. In reality, the 45-minute bus ride to campus meant paying around $80 a month for a transit pass, the house had no central heat so she spent extra on space heaters and higher electric bills in winter, and the Wi-Fi was so unreliable she often ended up buying coffee just to use a café connection for online lectures.

On paper, her rent was lower. In real life, that "deal" cost her more money, more time, and a lot of stress.

Next up, we are going to talk about viewings, paperwork, and how to protect yourself before you sign anything.

BEFORE YOU SIGN THAT DOTTED LINE

Seeing a place in person is not just about "Do I like the vibe?" It is your chance to spot problems, gather evidence, and decide whether this rental is going to support you or drain you.

A systematic viewing checklist sounds boring. It is also one of the most financially protective habits you can have as a renter.

STRUCTURAL AND SAFETY CHECKS

Start with the basics that keep you safe and comfortable. Flip the light switches in every room. Lights flickering or not turning on can hint at electrical issues.

Turn on faucets and the shower to check water pressure and temperature. A sad drizzle every morning gets old very fast.

If you can, test the heating and AC. If it is not possible on the day, at least ask how they work and whether there have been issues. Heating and cooling problems are expensive and miserable to live with.

Check that windows open and close properly and that all door and window locks actually work. Security is not something you want to discover is bad after you move in. Look for smoke detectors and carbon monoxide detectors and ask if they are tested regularly.

Scan for signs of mold, damp patches, water stains on ceilings, or pests. Musty smells, flaking paint, and suspicious dark spots in corners are not "quirks," they are warnings.

DOCUMENTATION ESSENTIALS

Your camera roll is your best friend here. Before you move in—or at your viewing if you are serious about the place—take photos and short videos of any damage: scratched floors, cracked tiles, chipped paint, dented doors, stained carpets.

Turn on the oven, washer, dryer, and any included appliances during the viewing if possible. Do they actually work, or do they just *exist*?

Make a note of exactly what comes with the place: furniture, appliances, blinds, light fixtures. The more specific your list, the easier it is to argue if anything disappears or gets misattributed to you later.

Clarify what is included in the rent and what you have to supply yourself. Do you need your own microwave? Will you be buying a mattress? This affects both your move-in budget and your stress levels.

PRACTICAL LIVING CONSIDERATIONS

Bring a tape measure or measuring app if you can. Check that your bed, desk, and storage will actually fit without turning your room into a human Tetris level.

Check your cell signal inside the apartment, not just on the street. A dead zone in your bedroom might mean relying completely on Wi-Fi for basic calls and texts. Then, test the Wi-Fi if you can, or ask current tenants how reliable it is.

Listen for noise: neighbors, traffic, nearby businesses, trains. If possible, swing by the area at a different time of day or at night to see what it is *really* like.

Michael did a five-minute tour of an apartment, decided it was "good enough," and signed on the spot because he loved the location. On move-in day, he discovered the shower had almost no pressure, the heater in his room never kicked on, and the washing machine did not work. Because he had not asked questions or documented anything, his landlord insisted those problems were his responsibility.

His friend Sarah, on the other hand, showed up to her viewing with a simple checklist and took photos of every pre-existing issue. When she moved out, the landlord tried to keep part of her deposit for "damage." Her photos told a different story, and she got the full amount back.

Next, we are going to zoom in even further on lease agreements, deposits, and what your rights actually look like on paper.

SPOTTING DREAM RENTALS AND DODGING DISASTERS

The last layer of protection before you commit to a place is what you ask—and who you ask. The listing tells one story. The landlord and current tenants can tell you the rest, if you know how to prompt them.

Just like reading credit card terms saved you from traps in Chapter 3, asking clear housing questions can save you from moving into a disaster with a fresh coat of paint.

ESSENTIAL LANDLORD QUESTIONS

Ask how maintenance works. Who do you contact when something breaks? How quickly do they usually respond? A good landlord or management company will have a clear process and realistic timelines.

Ask about rent increases. Is the rent fixed for the duration of your lease? Do they typically raise it each year, and by how much? This matters if you are thinking of staying more than one year.

Find out how they handle the security deposit. Where is it held? When do you get it back? In many places, deposits have to be kept in a specific way and returned within a set timeframe after you move out. If a landlord seems vague or annoyed by this question, that is not a great sign.

Ask what happens if a roommate moves out mid-lease. Does the total rent stay the same and you are all responsible for covering it, or does the landlord help fill the empty room? Are you allowed to find a replacement yourself?

QUESTIONS FOR CURRENT TENANTS

Whenever possible, talk to someone who actually lives there. If the landlord or agent hovers, ask politely if you can chat with the tenants alone for a moment.

Ask how it really is to live there. Is the place generally comfortable? Are there ongoing issues, like constant plumbing problems or noise from a nearby bar?

Ask how responsive the landlord is. When something breaks, do they fix it quickly, or do they ghost you for weeks?

Ask what the neighborhood is like at different times. Daytime, late at night, weekends. How is parking? Do they feel safe walking home?

And then the big one: Would you recommend living here to a friend? The pause before they answer usually tells you more than the words do.

MAJOR RED FLAGS TO AVOID

Some signs should make you walk away, no matter how cute the kitchen is.

If a landlord pressures you to sign immediately—"I have three other people lined up, you need to decide right now"—they might be hiding problems or just banking on you panicking.

If they refuse to give you a written lease, want cash-only payments with no receipts, or avoid simple legal questions, that is not "chill," that is unsafe.

If they dodge questions about repairs or act offended when you ask about their response times, expect future arguments when something breaks.

If current tenants seem tense, shut down your questions, or clearly want to say more but will not in front of the landlord, pay attention. Their discomfort is data.

REAL EXAMPLES

Isabella almost signed for a gorgeous apartment with exposed brick and fairy lights in the photos. Before committing, she asked if she could talk to one of the current tenants alone. Once the door closed, the tenant admitted that the boiler broke regularly in winter, the landlord took weeks to fix anything, and the upstairs neighbors hosted loud parties most weekends. That five-minute chat saved Isabella from a year of cold showers and no sleep.

Marcus, on the other hand, found his current place after talking to the person moving out. They happily listed the pros, mentioned a few small quirks, said the landlord fixed things quickly, and finished with, "Honestly, I'd stay if I wasn't graduating." That is the kind of green flag you want.

Your housing choice shapes your college experience just as much as your class schedule or major. Take the time to understand your options, factor in more than just rent, and treat viewings and questions as part of your financial life, not just your social life.

Once you have found a place that works on paper *and* in reality, the next step is learning how leases, deposits, and renter rights protect you—so you can sign with confidence instead of crossed fingers.

5

Leases, Landlords, and Deposit Drama

LEASE JARGON DECODED FOR REAL PEOPLE

You have picked a place to live. Congrats. Now comes the part where someone hands you a ten-page document written in a language that looks like English but feels like a trap.

That document is your lease. It is the rulebook for your living situation: what you agree to do, what your landlord agrees to do, and what happens if either side drops the ball. It is not exciting reading, but it is absolutely worth understanding *before* your signature goes anywhere near it.

Most leases are written in maximum-legalese, which makes normal people want to skim and hope for the best. Instead, let's break down the key phrases you are most likely to see so you can read with confidence instead of panic.

At the top level, there are two main types of rental agreements: fixed-term and month-to-month.

• A fixed-term lease locks you in for a specific period—often 12 months for students or for the length of the academic year. You are responsible for the rent for that full period.

• A month-to-month lease keeps rolling every month until someone gives proper notice (often 30 days). These offer more flexibility but sometimes come with higher rent or easier termination for both sides.

. . .

Student housing often uses fixed-term leases that match the school year. Off-campus apartments can be either, so always check.

You might also see the phrase "joint and several liability" if you are sharing with roommates. This is the scary one. It means that every person on the lease is responsible for the *entire* rent, not just "their share." If your roommate vanishes halfway through the year, the landlord does not chase "their half"—they can legally come after *any* of you for the whole amount.

This is where your emergency fund and backup plans from Chapter 2 matter. Roommate drama can turn into real money problems very quickly.

Break clauses and notice periods explain how you can end the lease early and how much heads-up you have to give. Some leases let you break early with a penalty or if you find an acceptable replacement tenant. Others do not let you leave at all until the end date unless everyone (including the landlord) agrees. Notice periods are usually 30 or 60 days, and they must be followed exactly or you can get charged extra rent.

Your security deposit is usually around one month of rent, sometimes more. It is there to cover unpaid rent or damage beyond normal wear and tear. In many states, landlords must keep that money in a separate account and give you an itemized list of any deductions when you move out.

Because most students do not have much income or a long credit history, landlords often ask for a guarantor—usually a parent or close family member—who promises to pay if you do not. This is not symbolic. It is a real legal commitment, and missed rent can affect *their* credit, not just yours.

Ethan learned this the hard way. He thought he had found the perfect student house until he actually sat down and read the lease. Buried in the fine print was a clause that said if any roommate left early, the remaining tenants were responsible for that person's share until a replacement moved in.

Halfway through the year, one roommate transferred schools. Suddenly Ethan and the others were each paying an extra $200 a month. They did manage, but it made the rest of the year tight.

The lesson is simple and harsh:

Always read the entire lease, especially the parts about roommates and early move-outs.

Do not just skim for the rent amount and the move-in date. This document controls your life—and your wallet—for months. If something looks confusing, ask questions. If something looks unfair, ask whether it can be changed *before* you sign. Future you will be grateful you took the extra 20 minutes to understand what you were agreeing to.

Once you are comfortable with the jargon, you are in a much stronger position for Chapter 6, where we will talk about actually *living* with other humans without losing your mind (or your deposit).

YOUR MONEY AND LEGAL SAFETY NET

Your security deposit is one of the biggest up-front costs of renting—and one of the easiest places to lose money if you do not understand how it works.

Think of your deposit as a temporary loan to your landlord. It is still *your* money, just parked with them as insurance in case you trash the place or skip out on rent. If you treat the property reasonably well and pay what you owe, that money is supposed to come back to you at the end.

That matters a lot when every dollar in your student budget is already doing double duty.

In many US states, landlords must follow specific rules about deposits. Often they must:

- keep your deposit in a separate account,
- return it within a set number of days after you move out (for example, 14–30 days), and
- give you a written, itemized list of anything they are deducting for repairs or cleaning.

If they do not follow those rules, some states let you claim extra compensation. Local laws vary, so it is worth checking your city or state's basic tenant rights when you start renting. The big confusion point is what the deposit can legally cover.

Normal wear and tear—like slightly worn carpet, minor scuffs on walls, or faded paint from sunlight—generally should *not* come out of your deposit. Those are just signs that humans lived there. Damage beyond normal use—like big holes in the wall, broken doors, missing furniture, deep stains, or burns—can legitimately be deducted.

A helpful way to think about it:

If something would need to be replaced or repainted anyway after several years of normal use, that is usually wear and tear.

If it happened because someone dropped, spilled, punched, burned, or ignored basic care, that is damage.

Guarantors sit in the middle of all this. When your parent or family member signs as guarantor, they are agreeing to cover unpaid rent and sometimes damage costs if you do not. That is a serious favor. Make sure they see the lease, understand joint liability, and know exactly what they are promising.

The easiest way to protect yourself and your guarantor? Documentation.

On move-in day, before you unpack a single box, walk through the entire place and take photos and short videos of everything:

- floors, walls, ceilings
- inside closets and cabinets
- appliances, sinks, toilets, showers
- any stains, scratches, cracks, or weird patches you see

Then email those photos to your landlord or property manager with a polite note: "Here are move-in condition photos for Unit X as of [date]. Just wanted to document existing wear and tear." Now you have a timestamped record nobody can argue with later.

Patricia was grateful she did this. When she moved out after two years, her landlord tried to keep $300 of her deposit for "carpet cleaning and repainting." She was surprised—the apartment was tidy and she had not done anything wild in it.

Her secret weapon? Those move-in photos. They showed the carpet already had stains when she arrived. When she pushed back and attached the pictures, the landlord reduced the deduction and she got $250 back.

Without those photos, it would have been her word against theirs. With them, it was just math.

Knowing how deposits work—and how to defend yours—will matter even more when we get into roommate life in Chapter 6. Their behavior can affect your deposit too, so you will want every tool available to protect yourself.

MASTER LANDLORD COMMUNICATION WITH READY TEMPLATES

Your landlord is not your friend, your enemy, or your therapist. They are a business contact. Treating them like one is the fastest way to get things fixed and keep records that protect you if something goes wrong.

This connects to the communication skills we will dig deeper into in Chapter 10, but you can start right now with a simple rule: if it matters, put it in writing.

Texting is fine for quick updates ("just confirming I got the keys, thanks"), but important things—repairs, complaints, questions about the lease, issues with neighbors—should always go through email. Email creates a paper trail with dates, times, and exact wording.

Even if you talk on the phone, follow up with an email like:

"Thanks for speaking with me earlier about the leaking sink. Just to confirm, you'll be sending a plumber on Thursday afternoon. I'll make sure someone is home between 2–4 p.m. so they can get in."

Now, if something gets delayed or disputed later, you have proof of what was agreed.

When you contact your landlord about an issue, be:

- clear about what is wrong,
- specific about when it started and how serious it is, and
- reasonable about what you are asking for.

"Something's wrong with the heating" is vague.

"This week the heater in the living room stopped working. The thermostat is set to 70°F but the room stays around 60°F even after several hours. This started on [date]. Can you please arrange a repair in the next few days?" is much more useful.

At some point, you may need to escalate if nothing gets done. That might mean:

- contacting your school's student legal services or housing office,
- reaching out to a local tenant rights organisation, or
- checking your city or county's housing department for next steps.

Knowing where you would go for help *before* things go wrong makes emergencies less scary.

Marcus learned the power of proper communication by accident. When his shower started leaking through the kitchen ceiling, he texted his landlord: "shower's broken lol help." Nothing happened.

A week later, with the drip getting worse, he wrote a formal email instead:

"Dear Ms. Rivera,

I'm writing to report an urgent repair at [full address]. The shower in the main bathroom has developed a significant leak that is now dripping through the kitchen ceiling below. This started on [specific date] and has been getting worse each day.

Because this could cause water damage to the property, I'd really appreciate it if you could arrange for a plumber to assess and fix the problem within the next 48 hours. Please confirm you've received this email and let me know when the repair is scheduled.

Thank you,

Marcus [Last Name]"

He had a plumber booked within 24 hours. Same problem, completely different response.

The formal email made the issue sound as serious as it actually was, gave specific details and a requested timeframe, and quietly signaled, "I'm documenting this."

That last part often speeds things up a lot.

The more comfortable you get with this style of communication now, the easier it will be to handle roommate conflicts, job emails, and future "Hi, I'm reaching out about that bill..." moments.

BREAKDOWNS, BATTLES, AND BOND RECOVERY

Even with the best preparation, things go wrong: heaters die, landlords drag their feet, deposits "mysteriously" shrink. This is where all your habits—budgeting, documentation, calm emails—stop being hypothetical and start saving you real money.

Rule one: document everything.

- Take photos when you move in.
- Take photos when something breaks.
- Take photos when you move out.
- Keep all your emails in a folder.

If your landlord tries to claim you "never reported" a repair or that damage was your fault, you want timestamps and receipts, not just righteous emotions. Evidence beats arguments every time.

Rule two: know basic repair expectations.

Laws vary by state, but generally landlords are required to keep your place in a safe, habitable condition. That usually means dealing quickly with:

- no heat in winter
- serious leaks
- broken toilets or plumbing
- electrical hazards
- pest infestations

Emergency issues should get attention fast—often within 24 hours or a couple of days. Less urgent problems, like a broken closet door or chipped paint, may take longer. If weeks go by with no response to a serious issue, that is when you start looking at tenant support resources in your area.

Rule three: use the deposit dispute process when you need it.

If your landlord sends you a move-out statement with deductions you do not agree with, you are allowed to push back. Start by replying with a calm email, attaching your photos, and explaining why you think specific charges are unfair.

If that does not work and the amount is large enough to matter, you can look into:

- free legal clinics through your college,
- local tenant unions or housing nonprofits, or
- small claims court if it comes to that.

Sarah learned this during move-out from her second-year place. The landlord tried to keep $400 from her deposit for "various damages" that she knew were either pre-existing or just normal wear and tear.

Luckily, she had:

- move-in photos showing the original condition,
- emails where she had reported minor issues earlier in the year, and
- move-out photos showing she had left the place clean.

She wrote a detailed response, attached her evidence, and when the landlord refused to budge, she contacted a local tenant help clinic. With their guidance, she pushed the issue further. In the end, she recovered $320 of the disputed $400.

Some of her roommates, who had not bothered with photos or emails, lost their entire deposits without much recourse. The difference was not who "deserved" it more. The difference was who had proof.

RECAP AND ACTION STEPS

Leases are the boring rulebooks that quietly control your housing, your money, and sometimes your stress levels.

- They spell out your responsibilities and your rights.
- Your deposit is your money on hold—not a tip for your landlord.

- Professional communication gets better results than casual texts.
- Documentation is your shield when things go wrong.

Most landlords are just people running a business. Many will treat you fairly if you treat them professionally. Knowing your rights and building good habits just closes the loopholes that the occasional bad landlord might try to exploit.

A few concrete moves you can make right now:

- Before signing any lease, read the whole thing and write down questions. Ask about joint liability, early move-out, and how repairs work.
- On move-in day, take photos and videos of every room, then email them to your landlord as a record.
- Create a "Housing" folder in your email and save every message between you and your landlord there.
- After every important phone call, send a quick summary email: "Just to confirm what we discussed…"

Once you have this legal and money safety net in place, you are ready for the next level of real life: the human beings you are sharing walls, dishes, and fridge shelves with. Even the best lease in the world cannot fix roommate chaos—so that is where we are heading next.

6

Roommates, Chores, and Not Hating Each Other

BUILDING YOUR DEFENSE BEFORE BATTLE BEGINS

Living with strangers can feel like tiptoeing through a minefield blindfolded—especially right after you've signed that lease from the last chapter and handed over your security deposit. The goal is not to avoid all conflict. The goal is to set clear expectations from day one so everyone knows what "normal" looks like in your shared space.

Think of ground rules as roommate insurance: boring to create, priceless when things get messy.

Most roommate disasters start because everyone assumes their version of "normal" is universal. Your idea of "I'll do the dishes soon" might mean "within 24 hours." Your roommate's version might mean "as soon as I put my fork down." Neither is wrong. They're just different—and nobody bothered to say that out loud.

ESSENTIAL GROUND RULES TO TACKLE IN WEEK ONE

• Quiet hours and noise levels – When does the apartment need to be calm for sleep or studying? Are headphones required after a certain time?

• Kitchen and common area cleanliness – How long can dishes stay in the sink? Who cleans what, and how often?

• Guest policies – How much notice do people need for overnight guests? Are there limits on how many nights in a row someone's partner can basically live on the couch?

• Bill splitting and payment dates – Who's paying which bill, and when does everyone need to send their share each month?

• Personal space boundaries – Is any food "free-for-all"? Can people borrow clothes or electronics? What's completely off-limits?

Create a written roommate agreement in your first week together. It doesn't need to be notarized or live in a fancy binder. A shared Google Doc or a note in your phones works. The point is to get everyone's expectations out in the open *before* people get comfortable assuming their habits are "obvious."

Felix moved into a four-bedroom shared house in September. By November, the vibe was toxic. One roommate left dishes for days, another brought dates home without warning, and nobody could agree on when to turn the heat on or who should pay extra when the bill spiked.

The issue wasn't that they were terrible people; it was that they were all operating off invisible rulebooks.

When Felix suggested a house meeting, everyone was secretly relieved. It turned out they all wanted the same thing: a reasonably clean kitchen, a heads-up about overnight guests, and not arguing over utilities. They just hadn't said any of it out loud.

Schedule regular check-ins, maybe once a month. A quick, "Hey, how's everyone feeling about the house stuff?" conversation can keep tiny irritations from becoming World War Fridge. Address issues while they're still small enough to talk about without yelling.

You don't have to be best friends with your roommates. You're building a functional living system that lets everyone breathe. Once that's in place, the next chapter will dive into kitchen basics so you can feed yourself without wrecking your Chapter 2 budget.

SMART STRATEGIES FOR SPLITTING SHARED COSTS

Money fights can poison a good living situation faster than a forgotten takeout container rotting in the back of the fridge.

You got through the lease and deposit from Chapter 5; now comes the everyday money juggling: shared costs. The goal is a system that feels fair, is simple to follow, and doesn't depend on one responsible person chasing everyone every month.

Transparency prevents resentment. Clear processes prevent the "Oh, I didn't realize you'd already paid that" routine. When people keep "accidentally" missing payments, you don't need better roommates—you need better systems.

Shared cost categories to sort out early:

- Utilities – Electricity, gas, water, trash, internet, and any shared streaming services
- Household supplies – Toilet paper, cleaning products, dish soap, trash bags
- Shared food items – Milk, bread, oil, salt, spices, coffee if everyone drinks it
- Maintenance basics – Light bulbs, basic repair items, pest control if needed

Use bill-splitting tools like Splitwise, Venmo groups, or even a shared house account everyone contributes to monthly. These tools keep the math honest and the records clear, so nobody has to screenshot their bank app as "proof" every time. Your budgeting skills from Chapter 2 plug in here: you're now tracking *both* your personal spending and your share of household costs.

Decide what's shared and what's individual before the first grocery run. Paper towels and toilet paper? Shared. Brand-name almond butter, specialty snacks, or $7 kombucha? Probably personal.

This one decision saves you from arguing about whether everyone should pay for one person's gluten-free pasta or fancy coffee habit.

Be honest about different budget levels. Some students have strong family support. Others are surviving on loans and a part-time job. If one roommate genuinely can't afford organic everything or top-tier internet, talk about it. Maybe you downgrade the grocery plan, or the person who wants the premium option covers the extra.

Elizabeth found this out the awkward way. Her roommate started buying organic everything with the "house grocery budget" and assumed everyone was fine splitting the bill. Meanwhile, Elizabeth's loan money was stretched thin, and fifteen-dollar olive oil felt like a personal attack.

The fix was simple. They switched to individual grocery shopping, with a small shared pot for basics like milk, bread, and cleaning supplies. But it took one uncomfortable conversation to get there.

Now, Elizabeth always recommends talking through:

- how you'll shop,
- what counts as shared, and
- what everyone's price comfort zone is

before anyone starts filling a cart. Some houses love big group grocery trips. Others prefer, "You buy your stuff, I buy mine, we split basics." Some rotate who buys shared items each week.

The exact method matters less than everyone agreeing to the same rules. The next chapter will help you actually cook the food you're paying for—so it doesn't sit in the fridge while you order takeout for the fourth time this week.

HOUSE RULES THAT ACTUALLY STICK

The fastest route to a hostile apartment is letting everyone's different cleanliness and lifestyle standards smash into each other with zero structure.

You've signed the lease (Chapter 5), figured out the money systems, and now you need house rules that work in real life, not just in a group chat.

What feels "reasonable" with noise, mess, or social life varies person to person. Most conflicts disappear when you swap fuzzy expectations for clear agreements.

Vague rules like "keep it clean" are useless. Clean *how*? Clean *when*? Clean *to whose standards*?

Same with "be respectful." Respectful to you might be "no

loud TV after 10 p.m." Respectful to your roommate might be "I wear headphones, so I'm good."

House rules to make specific:

- Cleaning responsibilities and timing – Who cleans what, how often, and what "done" actually looks like
- Noise levels and quiet hours – What time the apartment needs to be calm on weeknights, what's okay on weekends, where calls and loud gaming happen
- Guest policies and social boundaries – Overnight guests, parties, people crashing on the couch, and how much notice everyone needs
- Personal space and borrowing rules – Who can use what, what needs explicit permission, and what is completely off-limits

Create a realistic cleaning schedule that accounts for people's lives. Don't assign "Saturday morning kitchen deep clean" to the roommate who works double shifts every weekend. Some people love doing a big weekly clean; others prefer small tasks daily. Rotate jobs so no one is permanently the Toilet Person while someone else only ever "takes out trash."

Set clear quiet hours and common area rules. For example: "No loud music or TV in the living room after 11 p.m. on weeknights; after midnight on weekends," or "During finals week, the living room is quiet after 9 p.m. for studying." That gives everyone something solid to point to instead of arguing about vibes.

Guest policies should balance personal freedom with everyone's comfort. Decide:

- How many nights a week partners or friends can stay over
- Whether guests can use the kitchen and shower freely
- How much notice everyone needs before a party or big hangout

Some people like a full social house. Others need mental notice before they walk into a surprise group in the living room. Clear agreements let both types exist without hating each other.

Marcus thought he was being chill by having friends over for drinks twice a week. To him, that was "normal college life." His roommates, however, felt like they never had a night where they could just flop on the couch without having to socialize or hide in their rooms.

Once they talked, they agreed that:

• on weeknights, gatherings would end by 10 p.m.

• weekend parties needed 48 hours' notice in the group chat

Suddenly, everyone could plan. Marcus still had his social life, and his roommates could choose to join or disappear to a friend's place if they wanted.

Write your house rules down and revisit them every month or two. What works in September might not work in March when everyone is tired, stressed, and surviving off caffeine and deadlines.

DEFUSING HOUSEHOLD BOMBS BEFORE THEY DETONATE

Most roommate blowups don't come out of nowhere. They start small: one annoyance, then another, then another. Nobody says anything, resentment piles up, and eventually someone loses it over a spoon in the sink.

Learning how to speak up early—and knowing *how* to say things—turns conflict from a meltdown into a manageable conversation.

Think of conflict resolution like regular maintenance on your living space. Fixing a tiny leak now is way easier than dealing with a collapsed ceiling later. Same idea, fewer buckets.

Key communication strategies:

• Use "I" statements and focus on behavior, not personality

◦ "I've noticed the kitchen hasn't been cleaned after people cook this week" works better than "You're disgusting."

• Talk about issues within 48 hours, not four weeks later

◦ The longer you wait, the more emotional weight attaches to the problem.

• Bring solutions, not just complaints

◦ Suggest schedule changes, trade-offs, or small tweaks that might fix things.

• Choose your battles

. . .

Not every small irritation needs a full meeting. Save serious talks for things that actually affect your sleep, safety, or ability to function.

Hope was losing her mind because her roommate kept leaving wet laundry in the washer for days. It made everything smell gross and backed up everyone else's loads.

Instead of venting to other roommates or leaving angry notes, she knocked and said:

"Hey, I've noticed laundry's been sitting in the washer for a couple of days sometimes. Could we agree that whoever's using it moves stuff to the dryer within 12 hours? I can text you a reminder when I need to use it if that helps."

The whole conversation took under two minutes. Her roommate was embarrassed, apologized, and started setting timers on his phone. Problem solved. No drama required.

Hope realized something huge: most people are not villains. They're just on autopilot. Clear, calm feedback flips the switch.

Sometimes, though, issues reveal deeper incompatibility. If someone consistently ignores agreements, refuses to compromise, or blows up when confronted, you might need to think longer-term—like not renewing the lease with them next year.

But most roommate problems are not personality disasters. They're expectation problems. And expectations can be fixed.

RECAP AND ACTION STEPS

Living successfully with roommates is not about finding perfect people who magically match your standards. It's about building clear systems for messy humans.

You:

- set ground rules early instead of waiting for a crisis
- create simple, fair money systems for shared costs
- agree on cleaning standards, noise rules, and guest expectations
- and practice bringing up problems while they're still small

. . .

A few practical moves you can make right now:

- Schedule a house meeting within your first two weeks of living together
- Set up your bill-splitting system (apps, shared account, or both)
- Create a cleaning schedule and agree on quiet hours and guest rules
- Pick one tiny annoyance and practice addressing it calmly using "I" statements

Once your people and systems are in place, you're ready for the next level: learning how to actually feed yourself without setting your budget—or your kitchen—on fire.

7

Cooking So You Don't Live on Instant Noodles

KITCHEN HAZARDS THAT COULD HURT YOU

Your kitchen is not out to kill you... but it *can* absolutely injure you if you treat it like a chaotic science lab. Most kitchen accidents happen when people are rushed, distracted, or have no idea how their equipment works—which describes pretty much every college student during midterms running on caffeine and vibes.

A few simple rules will keep you from slicing fingers, burning hands, or setting off the fire alarm so often your neighbors know you by name.

SHARP OBJECTS AND HOT SURFACES

Sharp knives are actually *safer* than dull ones. Dull blades make you press harder, which makes slipping more likely. Keep your knife clean and sharp, and when you chop, curl your fingertips under like a claw so your knuckles guide the blade instead of your fingertips volunteering as a sacrifice.

Always cut away from your body, not toward it, and never just toss knives into drawers where you can grab the blade by accident. Use a knife block, magnetic strip, or at least lay them flat and visible.

Hot surfaces are sneaky. Pan handles heat up faster than you think, especially metal ones. Use a dry oven mitt or kitchen towel when you move anything on the stove or out of the oven. Turn pot and pan handles inward so nobody bumps them while walking past.

And remember: glass and ceramic dishes stay hot long after they're out of the oven. Just because they're no longer glowing doesn't mean they're safe to grab with bare hands.

OIL AND GREASE SAFETY

Hot oil demands respect.

Never walk away from a pan of oil heating on the stove. If the oil starts smoking, that's your cue: turn off the heat immediately and step back. Do *not* throw water on it. Ever. Water plus hot oil equals explosive splatter and a potential grease fire.

Know where your smoke alarms and fire extinguisher are in your apartment. Keep a lid or a flat baking sheet nearby so you can cover a small grease fire and smother it. A damp kitchen towel can help for tiny flare-ups, but water should *never* be poured onto hot oil.

Jace learned this in week two of freshman year. He was making fries in a pan of hot oil while video chatting with his girlfriend. He got distracted, the oil started smoking heavily, and his brain tried to panic.

Then he remembered his roommate's advice:

Turn the burner off. Step back. Let it cool.

His fries were ruined, but his eyebrows and apartment survived.

EQUIPMENT BASICS

Before you start pressing random buttons on that oven, microwave, or blender, take five minutes to figure out how it actually works.

Different ovens run hotter or cooler than their settings. Some microwaves have hot spots that will melt cheese into lava in one corner and leave the rest frozen. That fancy blender your roommate brought from home may have safety locks you need to engage before it turns on.

When in doubt, ask someone who knows, or quickly look up the brand and model online instead of winging it.

Keep your workspace clear while you cook. Wipe up spills as they happen—water, oil, or food on the floor plus a rushing student equals a twisted ankle and a very embarrassing story. Cluttered counters also increase your chances of knocking something sharp or hot onto yourself.

EMERGENCY PREPAREDNESS

You don't need to be a doctor, but basic first aid knowledge is non-negotiable.

• For burns, run cool water over the area for at least 20 minutes. Not ice. Ice can damage skin further.

• For cuts, apply firm pressure with a clean cloth or paper towel until the bleeding slows. If it won't stop, or the cut is deep, you need medical attention.

Keep a simple first aid kit in the apartment with bandages, antiseptic wipes, and pain relievers. Make sure everyone knows where it lives.

And remember your Chapter 6 communication skills: have a quick house chat about kitchen safety. Agree on fire extinguisher locations, what to do in an emergency, and who to call. It's a lot less awkward to talk safety *before* something catches fire than while you're standing outside with the fire department.

STUDENT KITCHEN SURVIVAL ESSENTIALS

You do *not* need a Pinterest-perfect kitchen to cook real food. You just need a small set of reliable tools and some basic ingredients that can morph into lots of different meals.

Your goal: the smallest possible amount of stuff that lets you cook the largest possible number of things.

ESSENTIAL TOOLS THAT ACTUALLY MATTER

You can survive almost any student cooking situation with:

- one good knife
- one cutting board
- one medium saucepan
- one frying pan

- one wooden spoon or spatula
- one can opener
- a set of measuring cups/spoons

That's it. Seriously.

One sharp, medium-sized chef's knife (or Santoku) from a discount store will handle most chopping jobs. Pair it with a plastic cutting board you can scrub easily and replace when it gets too gross.

Your saucepan should be big enough to boil pasta, cook rice, or make simple soups.

Your frying pan should feel balanced in your hand and lie flat on the burner. Nonstick is easier to clean, but a regular pan works as long as you use some oil and don't burn everything on high heat.

You don't get extra adult points for owning five pans you never use. Start small. You can always add later.

PANTRY STAPLES FOR ENDLESS POSSIBILITIES

A tiny list of pantry basics can carry you through a ridiculous number of meals:

- pasta
- rice
- canned tomatoes
- cooking oil (olive or vegetable)
- salt and pepper
- garlic
- onions
- eggs

Pasta and rice are your base. Canned tomatoes become pasta sauce, soup, or the start of a cheap "whatever's in the fridge" stew. Oil helps you cook *and* dress salads. Garlic and onions rescue almost any dish from tasting like cardboard and last for weeks when stored in a cool, dry place.

Eggs are your secret superfood: scrambled, fried, boiled, added to rice, tucked into wraps, mixed into pasta… they show up everywhere and keep you full longer than plain carbs.

SPICES THAT TRANSFORM EVERYTHING

A few cheap spices turn "student food" into "okay wait, this is actually good":

- paprika
- cumin
- dried mixed herbs (like Italian seasoning)
- chili flakes

Paprika adds warmth and color to potatoes, veggies, or chicken.

Cumin gives instant depth to rice, eggs, and roasted vegetables.

Dried herbs save you from having five half-dead bunches of fresh herbs in the fridge.

Chili flakes let you choose your own spice adventure—just a tiny pinch can shift the entire dish.

Charlotte arrived at college armed with nothing but a kettle, a mug, and big sandwich energy. After three weeks of cold meals and microwaved sadness, she spent about thirty dollars at a discount store: one knife, one pot, one pan, one cutting board.

Suddenly she could make real pasta with sauce, scrambled eggs, basic stir-fries, and soup. Her kitchen still looked nothing like her parents' at home, but she realized something important:

Fewer tools forced her to get creative—and that was enough to make grown-up meals on a student budget.

Those basics are a one-time investment that pays off every time you choose to cook instead of ordering takeout. In Chapter 8, we'll talk about keeping those tools clean and working so they actually last.

EFFORTLESS NUTRITIOUS MEALS ANYONE CAN NAIL

These are not "impress your food-blogger friend" kind of recipes. They're "I'm tired, broke, and need real food that isn't cereal" meals. Each one teaches you a simple pattern you can remix endlessly.

One-pot wonder meals

One-pot meals are the heroes of student cooking: fewer dishes, less effort, more food.

Think:

• pasta + canned tomatoes + veggies + seasoning

• rice + whatever protein you have + veggies + sauce

For basic pasta with stuff

1 Boil pasta according to the package.

2 Drain it.

3 Dump it back in the pot with canned tomatoes, any chopped veggies, and seasoning.

4 Stir until everything is hot and happy.

Rice works similarly. Cook it plain, then mix in:

• leftover meat,

• frozen veggies,

• a spoonful of butter or oil, and

• salt and pepper

You can't really "ruin" a one-pot meal. You just adjust it next time: more salt, different veg, extra cheese.

The beauty is flexibility:

• Leftover veggies? Toss them in.

• Found random cheese? Grate it on top.

• No fresh vegetables? Frozen ones are cheap, easy, and often better than wilted "fresh" produce.

Egg-based meals for any time

Eggs are the student MVP: breakfast, lunch, dinner, 1 a.m. snack.

Easy ideas:

• scrambled eggs on toast

• a simple omelet with cheese and veggies

• fried rice with an egg stirred in at the end

Scrambled eggs get more interesting when you add cheese, chopped tomato, leftover spinach, or herbs. Omelets are just scrambled eggs you stop stirring and fold in half.

For fried rice:

1 Heat oil in your pan.

2 Add leftover rice and veggies.

3 Push everything to one side, crack in an egg, scramble it, then mix it all together.

Suddenly leftover rice is a new meal, not sad fridge history.

Assembly meals that barely need cooking

Some days you don't want to "cook" as much as "assemble things with heat involved." That still counts.

Easy assembly ideas:

• loaded baked potatoes

• wraps with hummus, veggies, and whatever protein you have

• beans on toast with melted cheese

Baked potatoes sound fancy until you realize the microwave can do most of the work. Scrub the potato, poke it with a fork a few times, microwave 8–10 minutes (turn halfway), then finish in the oven or toaster oven if you want a crisp skin. Top with beans, cheese, leftover veggies, or just butter and salt.

Kevin was convinced he was doomed to a life of toast and instant noodles until his roommate taught him "pasta with stuff." Boil pasta. Drain it. Add canned tomatoes and whatever veg is lying around. Season with salt and pepper. That was it. Not Instagram-worthy, but hot, filling, and contained actual nutrients. Once Kevin understood the formula—carb + sauce + "stuff"—he started experimenting. Frozen peas, leftover chicken, cheese, spinach. Six months later, he was "the one who cooks" in the apartment.

These meals use cheap ingredients well and protect your budget from random takeout. The skills you're building now will quietly save you money for years. Next up in Chapter 8: cleaning up without turning your kitchen into a crime scene.

SMART KITCHEN PREP THAT PAYS OFF

Batch cooking sounds like something fitness influencers do on Sundays, but really it's just "make more now so you can be lazy later."

Future You will be tired. Future You will be tempted by overpriced campus food. Batch cooking is how Present You takes care of Future You.

BATCH COOKING BASICS

When you cook, double it. Eat one portion now and save the rest.

• Store leftovers in the fridge if you'll eat them within 2–3 days.

• Freeze extra portions if you want backup meals for later in the month.

Foods that batch-cook well:

• soups
• stews
• pasta dishes
• rice bowls
• chili
• casseroles

You're not adding a whole extra hour in the kitchen. You're just using a bigger pot and a slightly longer simmer so you get multiple meals out of one cooking session.

WHAT WORKS AND WHAT DOESN'T

Not everything loves a second life.

Great reheaters:

• soups and stews
• curries
• rice dishes
• tomato-based sauces

Often these taste *better* the next day because the flavors have had time to develop.

Fussy reheaters:

• roasted veggies (best reheated in the oven, not microwave)

• dishes with a lot of dairy (sauces might separate but can usually be stirred back together)

Bad batch-cook candidates:

• salads
• sandwiches
• anything crunchy that's supposed to stay crispy

For those, batch-cook the components instead: cook chicken, roast vegetables, make a big pot of rice—then build fresh bowls or wraps as needed.

LEFTOVER TRANSFORMATION TECHNIQUES

The real magic is learning to see leftovers as ingredients, not punishment.

• Roast chicken becomes chicken sandwiches, quesadillas, or pasta topping.

• Extra rice turns into fried rice or a rice bowl with eggs and veggies.

• Leftover pasta becomes pasta salad with a little oil, vinegar, and chopped veg.

• Cooked vegetables get tossed on baked potatoes, into omelets, or into soup.

Sophie used to cook from scratch every single night. It sounded healthy and adult… until she realized she was burning an hour a day in the kitchen and still running out of food mid-week.

Her older sister suggested Sunday batch cooking. Now Sophie spends about two hours making a big pot of chili and cooking extra rice. That gives her four nights of easy, real meals. She scoops out a portion, warms it up, adds cheese or extra veggies, eats, and is done in ten minutes.

Her grocery budget goes further, and she's not panic-ordering delivery every time she has a late class or exam crunch.

If you live with roommates, this is where your Chapter 6 communication skills come in again. Coordinate fridge space, label your food clearly, and maybe even split batch-cooking duties—one person makes chili, another makes pasta bake, everyone shares a portion.

In Chapter 8, we'll tackle keeping your kitchen and tools clean enough that you actually *want* to cook in there. Because the best meal plan in the world dies if your sink is a disaster zone.

8

Cleaning, Laundry, and Not Ruining Your Stuff

YOUR MESS-FREE LIFE BLUEPRINT

You do *not* need to bleach your apartment every day, no matter what your 2 a.m. anxiety tells you. The real skill is knowing the difference between "clean enough to live and think in" and "reels-ready, spotless show home."

A realistic cleaning routine stops actual dirt from building up *and* saves you from those horrible, once-a-month, six-hour scrubbing marathons.

Think of it like this:

• Daily-ish: make your bed, do the dishes, wipe kitchen counters, take out the trash when it's full

• Weekly: vacuum or sweep floors, clean the bathroom (toilet, sink, shower), change bed sheets, quick tidy of every room

• Monthly: deep clean kitchen appliances, wipe windows, declutter/organize closets and drawers

Penelope ignored all of this for three weeks. By the time she noticed, her shower had mold, her sink was a science experiment, and her dishes had evolved into a new ecosystem. Her roommates were not amused.

Now she spends about 30 minutes a week doing small, boring jobs—and magically never has to sacrifice an entire weekend to cleaning again.

LAUNDRY WITHOUT DRAMA

That mountain of clothes in the corner? It's not "floor storage." It's laundry.

Washing machines are simple, but they absolutely *can* destroy your stuff if you ignore a few basics. The goal is clean clothes, not doll-sized sweaters and tie-dyed underwear you didn't order.

Start with three basic piles:

- whites
- darks
- delicates / "nicer stuff"

This is not old-fashioned overkill. It's how you stop your socks from turning pink and your black jeans from bleeding all over everything else.

Before you hit start:

- Check every pocket. Every. Single. One. Your student ID, earbuds, and crumpled twenty will thank you.
- Use cold water for most loads. It's cheaper, better for the planet, and much less likely to shrink your clothes.
- Use about one capful of detergent. More soap does *not* equal cleaner clothes. It just leaves residue.

Harrison found out the hard way that his expensive wool sweater was not built for a hot wash and a trip through the dryer. It came out roughly the size of a teddy bear outfit.

Now he reads clothing labels and sends truly nice pieces to the dry cleaner when needed. Some clothes really do need professional care, and pretending they don't tends to end in heartbreak.

THE ART OF NOT DESTROYING YOUR BELONGINGS

Your stuff costs money. Your budget (from earlier chapters) does not have a "replace everything I broke because I was careless" category.

Basic maintenance goes a long way:

• Clean crumbs and dust out of your laptop keyboard with compressed air.

• Don't leave cold, wet cups sitting on wooden furniture—hello, permanent rings.

• Store winter clothes properly in the summer instead of leaving them in a damp pile.

Set up quick, simple routines: wipe your desk once a week, put shoes on a mat, hang up coats instead of dropping them on the floor. Small habits now save you from big, expensive problems later.

FRESH SPACES FROM FLOOR TO CEILING

You don't need a whole closet full of cleaning products to have a decent apartment. A few solid basics do most of the work.

Think about multi-use products, not "one spray for every possible mood."

Useful basics:

• an all-purpose cleaner (for counters, tables, general grime)
• toilet cleaner
• glass cleaner (mirrors, windows, screens)
• microfiber cloths and sponges
• a toilet brush
• a vacuum and/or mop
• trash bags

Create a simple trash routine: empty it *before* it's overflowing, always use trash bags, and know your building's trash pickup or dumpster situation so bags don't sit around getting weird.

Robert thought "cleaning" meant relocating dirty dishes from sink to counter and calling it a day. At his landlord's inspection, years of ignored grease and bathroom grime showed up all at once, and his deposit was suddenly on life support.

After his more organized roommate showed him a basic routine—wipe surfaces, scrub the bathroom once a week, quickly mop the worst areas—Robert realized five minutes a day beats five hours of panic-cleaning the night before an inspection.

ROOM-BY-ROOM REALITY CHECK

Not every space needs equal attention. Some areas can coast for a bit. Others turn into health hazards if you ignore them.

The kitchen is priority number one. You cook where you eat. Food plus warmth plus time equals bacteria. Combine that with your new meal prep skills, and you'll see why a semi-clean kitchen matters.

Kitchen focus:

- Wipe counters after each use.
- Wash or at least rinse dishes within 24 hours.
- Wipe stove and appliances weekly.
- Do a fridge clean-out and wipe-down monthly. Mystery leftovers are not roommates.

The bathroom is next in line.

Quick daily-ish wipe-downs of the sink and surfaces stop gross buildup. A weekly scrub of the toilet, shower, and sink keeps things hygienic. And for the love of your future self: replace the toilet paper before it's completely gone. Nobody wants to discover the empty tube at the worst moment.

Living spaces and bedroom:

- Vacuum/sweep once a week.
- Dust shelves and surfaces once a month.
- Keep clutter at a level where you can see the floor and find your bed.

A reasonably tidy space makes it easier for your brain to focus —something that connects directly to the time management systems you'll build in the next chapter.

PREVENTION BEATS PANIC CLEANING

Good cleaning habits are basically damage control in advance.

- Use coasters so your furniture doesn't die an early death.
- Wipe up spills immediately instead of "later." Later equals stains.

• Keep your main cleaning products somewhere easy to grab so you don't have the excuse of "Ugh, it's too much effort."

Madison spilled red wine on the carpet during a study night, panicked, tossed a towel over it, and walked away. Three weeks later, the stain was part of the decor—and it cost her a chunk of her deposit.

Now she tackles spills right away and keeps basic stain remover on hand. It takes seconds and saves money.

Regular, small cleaning jobs take less total time than ignoring everything and then spending your entire Saturday doing damage control. Mess prevention buys you more time for studying, seeing friends, and living your life.

DECODE YOUR LAUNDRY LIKE A PRO

Laundry stays "simple" right up until your white socks turn pink or your favorite sweater shrinks to "American Girl doll" size. The good news is that most disasters are totally avoidable once you know a few basics.

Core rules:

• Sort by color: darks, lights, whites.

• Sort by weight: heavy jeans and towels separate from lightweight t-shirts.

• Wash new dark items alone the first time so they don't bleed all over everything else.

• When in doubt: cold water, gentle cycle, low heat in the dryer.

Do not overstuff the machine. Water and detergent need room to move around. Overloading just gives you a tightly packed ball of "kind of wet, kind of dirty."

Clean the lint filter on the dryer every load—it helps clothes dry faster and reduces fire risk.

Sophia learned the hard way when she tossed a new red shirt in with her white work tops and ended up with a load of pastel pink uniforms she couldn't wear on shift. She had to replace three shirts—an expensive lesson for a simple mistake.

Now she uses separate laundry baskets for lights and darks and always checks pockets for tissues, pens, and mystery objects before hitting start.

READING THOSE WEIRD LABEL SYMBOLS

Clothing tags are basically tiny instruction manuals written in code. Once you know the basics, they actually help you keep your clothes alive longer.

• A circle often means dry clean only.

• A tub/bucket symbol shows how to wash: look for dots inside (one dot = cool, three dots = hot).

• A square symbol tells you about drying. A square with a circle inside = tumble dry.

• Any symbol with a big X through it simply means "don't do this."

You don't need to memorize every variation, but recognizing dry clean only, cool wash, and no tumble dry will already save you money and heartbreak.

TIMING AND EFFICIENCY

Laundry should fit *around* your life, not completely hijack it.

Most wash cycles are about 30–45 minutes. Drying takes around 45–60 minutes, depending on fabric and load size. Plan a load before you start studying or gaming so you can swap it between things, not in the middle of something important.

Set a phone timer for when the machine will finish. Being "the person who leaves wet clothes in the washer for three hours" earns you instant enemy status in any shared laundry room. And those wet clothes? Musty, gross, and often needing a second wash.

Tiny systems like these—timers, routines, separate laundry baskets—are the same kind of systems we'll build on in the time management chapter. Little bits of organization stack up.

WHEN THINGS GO WRONG

Even if you do everything right, stuff happens.

• Shrunk sweater? Sometimes soaking it in cool water with a bit of hair conditioner and gently stretching it while damp can revive it a little.

• Color bleed? There are color-run remover products that can sometimes rescue a load, but prevention is cheaper.

Marcus learned this with his nice wool sweater. One hot wash cycle later, it barely fit over his forearm. Now he treats anything labeled "wool," "cashmere," or "delicate" like it's on a VIP list and double-checks care labels before washing.

Keep basic stain-removal rules in your back pocket:

- Cold water for blood and sweat
- Warm water + dish soap for most food and grease
- Act fast, *then* decide what to do next

The fewer clothing disasters you have, the less money you'll end up stealing from other parts of your carefully built budget.

STAIN DISASTERS MEET THEIR MATCH

Stains are inevitable. Permanent stains are optional. The difference is how fast you act and *what* you do first.

Simple emergency plan:

1 Act quickly.

2 Blot—don't scrub.

3 Treat before it dries.

Some quick go-tos:

- Cold water + blotting for blood and sweat.
- A sprinkle of salt followed by cold water for fresh red wine.
- Dish soap for oily/greasy stains.
- White vinegar for deodorant marks and some mystery stains.

Keep a small "stain kit" in your room:

- liquid dish soap
- white vinegar
- baking soda
- a couple of clean, light-colored cloths or old t-shirts

Marcus once spilled curry all down his white shirt right before a job interview. Instead of spiraling, he ran cold water through the spot and gently worked in a bit of dish soap. Then he threw it in for a quick wash. The stain vanished, he made the interview, and he got the job.

He walked out knowing two things: 1) he could handle emergencies, and 2) dish soap is magic.

THE SCIENCE BEHIND QUICK ACTION

Most stains are way easier to remove *before* they dry or get heated. Heat (from hot water or the dryer) often "sets" a stain into the fabric.

Rubbing aggressively just grinds the stain deeper into the fibers. Blotting soaks it up and pulls it outward.

For protein-based stains like blood, sweat, or egg, hot water literally cooks the proteins into the fabric. Cold water keeps them loose so you can wash them out. That's why "start cold" is almost always a smart move.

BUILDING YOUR MAINTENANCE MINDSET

Everything you're doing here—quick cleaning, smart laundry habits, stain triage—is the same skill we used in the cooking chapter: small, regular actions that save you from big, ugly problems later.

Think of it this way:

- Every plate you wash tonight is one less thing to hate tomorrow.
- Every stain you treat right away is money you don't have to spend replacing clothes.
- Every 10-minute tidy session is one less overwhelming, all-day clean-up.

You're building a maintenance mindset—taking care of your space and stuff so it can take care of you.

CHAPTER SUMMARY AND NEXT STEPS

You don't need to be a clean freak or laundry genius. You just need simple, repeatable systems:

- A basic cleaning routine spread over daily, weekly, and monthly tasks
- A small set of cleaning supplies that actually get used
- Laundry rules that protect your clothes instead of sacrificing them
- A quick reaction plan for stains and spills

Perfection is not the goal. Consistency is.

Your next moves:

• Sketch a weekly cleaning schedule that fits your real life (even 10–15 minutes a day makes a big difference).

• Grab the basics: all-purpose cleaner, a couple of microfiber cloths, toilet cleaner, and laundry detergent that works for your clothes.

• Practice sorting and running one proper load of laundry start to finish.

• Put together a tiny stain kit with dish soap, white vinegar, and a clean cloth so you're ready for the next accident.

With your space under control and your stuff taken care of, you're ready for the next big challenge: managing your time when nobody else is telling you what to do or when to do it.

9

Time Management When No One's Chasing You

DESIGNING YOUR BURNOUT-PROOF WEEKLY BLUEPRINT

In high school, your whole day was basically pre-loaded for you. You showed up around 8 AM, bounced from class to class until 3 PM, and adults handled most of the logistics: dinner, rides, appointments, even reminding you when to go to bed.

Now you're in college staring at an empty calendar like, "How is it 11 PM and I somehow did… nothing?" Meanwhile, other students look like they've unlocked a secret adulting cheat code.

College doesn't come with that built-in 8-to-3 structure. You have pockets of class time, random gaps, and a ton of "figure it out yourself." A weekly schedule isn't about filling every minute. It's about creating a rhythm that lets you study, work, live, and still sleep without burning out.

Think of your time the way we treated cleaning in the last chapter. You don't wait until your room is a disaster and then panic-clean for six hours. You use small, regular habits. Time management works the same way: less chaos, more patterns.

START WITH THE NON-NEGOTIABLES

Build your weekly blueprint from the stuff that's fixed. These are the things that happen whether you plan around them or not:

- classes, labs, and discussion sections
- work shifts or internships
- regular activities (exercise classes, therapy, club meetings)
- basic life tasks (grocery runs, laundry, weekly room reset)

Put these on your calendar first. They're your anchor points. Once those are in place, you can actually *see* how much free time you're working with instead of guessing and overcommitting.

BLOCK SCHEDULING BEATS MICROMANAGING

Resist the urge to plan every hour like a Tetris board. Instead, think in blocks of time.

For example:

- Mornings: focused work (readings, essays, problem sets)
- Afternoons: errands, group projects, lighter tasks
- Evenings: social stuff, clubs, low-energy homework, or chill time

You don't need "Write essay from 2:00–2:45 PM" on your calendar. You need "Deep work block, 2–4 PM." That gives you structure without making you feel like a robot who "failed" if you started at 2:07.

BUFFER TIME SAVES YOUR SANITY

Here's the secret nobody mentions: everything takes longer than you think.

- That "quick" grocery run? Turns into 45 minutes because you bump into people you know and stand in line forever.
- That 50-minute class? The professor talks right up to the hour, then answers questions, and suddenly you're ten minutes behind.

- Build buffer time between commitments. Leave gaps in your schedule for:
- conversations that run long
- assignments that take more brainpower than expected
- surprise "Hey, can you talk?" moments with friends

Tessa once color-coded her week down to 30-minute blocks: "answer emails," "quick grocery trip," "finish reading," "clean desk." It looked gorgeous. It did not survive contact with reality.

Within two weeks everything was running late, the plan kept exploding, and she felt like she was failing at time management.

So she zoomed out. Now she plans in two- to three-hour blocks and leaves Wednesday afternoons open as a flex zone for catch-up or spontaneous plans. Her schedule finally feels like support, not a trap—and she gets more done because she isn't constantly "behind."

Your weekly blueprint should feel like a helpful framework, not a punishment.

In the next chapter, you'll layer communication skills on top of this: emails, boundaries, and all the talking-to-humans that makes this coordination actually work.

MASTERING LIFE'S FIVE-BALL BALANCING ACT

On most days you're juggling:

- classes
- work
- social life
- family stuff
- basic adulting (laundry, cleaning, money, sleep)

It can feel like you're one dropped ball away from everything crashing.

Here's a reframe: perfect balance doesn't exist.

Real life runs on intentional imbalance. Some weeks are academics-heavy. Others are more social. Some are recovery weeks where you're mostly catching up on sleep and laundry. The point isn't to give everything equal time. It's to decide where your energy goes *on purpose*.

THINK IN SEASONS, NOT DAYS

Your semester has its own seasons:

- early weeks feel lighter
- midterms hit
- group projects and papers stack up
- finals turn everything into survival mode

During exam weeks, your social life shrinks. That's not you "failing at balance." That's you being strategic. Later, when workload dips, you can pour more time into friends, hobbies, jobs, or dating.

Tell people what "season" you're in.

"I'm in exam tunnel until Thursday, but I'm free Friday night" is way better than vanishing for two weeks and then feeling guilty about it.

MASTER THE ART OF ACTIVITY COMBINING

You can't create more hours in the day, but you *can* stack benefits.

Think about combinations like:

- study dates where you actually work, then hang out after
- walking catch-ups with friends instead of sitting in a lounge
- listening to recorded lectures or podcasts while doing laundry or basic cleaning

You're not trying to cram more into every second. You're being smart with overlap.

IDENTIFY YOUR NON-NEGOTIABLES

Some things are your personal "basic operating system": skip them long enough and everything else falls apart.

Your list might include:

- roughly seven hours of sleep most nights

- one proper, sit-down meal with another human each week
- some kind of movement (walks, gym, stretching, dance)
- regular check-ins with family or your closest people

Put these in your schedule *first*. These are stability points, not extras. Everything else fits around them.

Harrison was working fifteen hours a week at a café on top of a full course load. Every choice felt wrong: if he studied, he felt guilty for missing time with his girlfriend; if he hung out, he felt guilty for not working or studying.

His turning point came when he stopped pretending he could do everything, all the time. He started being honest:

"I'm working a ton this week; I can do coffee Saturday, not three hangouts."

"I'm wiped tonight; can we FaceTime tomorrow instead?"

His girlfriend appreciated the clarity more than half-present, stressed-out hangouts. His friends took his "no" less personally when they understood the context.

The goal isn't perfect juggling. It's conscious juggling.

BREAK THE FREEZE AND START MOVING

You know that moment when you have a huge assignment due… and suddenly deep-cleaning your desk feels urgent? Or you spend an hour curating the perfect study playlist and never actually study?

That's procrastination: doing *anything* except the thing.

Procrastination isn't proof you're lazy. A lot of the time, it's your brain saying, "This feels too big, too boring, or too unclear, so we're going to avoid it."

Instead of trying to crush procrastination with sheer willpower, make starting so small and easy that avoiding it takes more effort.

Same principle as your cleaning habits: you didn't overhaul your entire apartment daily; you built little routines that made order the default.

THE TWO-MINUTE MAGIC RULE

If a task takes less than two minutes, do it immediately:

- reply to that short email
- put that dish in the sink or dishwasher
- drop that deadline into your calendar

For bigger tasks, commit to just two minutes.

Two minutes won't finish a research paper, but it *will* get you through the hardest part: starting. Once the document is open and one sentence is written, your brain has shifted from "avoid" to "in progress."

MAKE STEPS RIDICULOUSLY SMALL

"Write essay" is not a task. It's a whole project.

Smaller versions look like:

- "open essay document and write one terrible intro sentence"
- "skim assignment sheet and highlight key requirements"
- "outline three main points"
- "Study for exam" becomes:
- "find notes for chapters one to three"
- "review first two pages of notes"

Your brain can handle "open the file" on a day when "ace the exam" feels impossible. Tiny steps create momentum, and momentum gets you through work in ways that brute force rarely does.

CREATE PRODUCTIVE PROCRASTINATION MENUS

You *will* procrastinate sometimes. That's fine. Give Future You better options than "scroll TikTok until the sun explodes."

Make a short list of "productive procrastination" tasks you can do when you're avoiding the Big Thing:

- organize class notes
- tidy your desk
- respond to non-urgent emails
- review flashcards
- update your to-do list or calendar

It's still procrastination, but your life moves forward instead of stalling.

Beth used to sit in front of her laptop for hours, "working" on a research paper while actually rearranging playlists and tabs. She eventually realized that whenever she resisted an assignment, it was because she didn't know where to start.

Now, when the avoidance feeling hits, she asks, "What's the tiniest possible step?"

Sometimes it's just opening the right article or writing one ugly sentence she fully plans to edit later. That little step snaps her out of freeze mode and gives her something to build on.

Momentum beats perfection every time.

SMART TOOLS THAT ACTUALLY HELP

College students are drowning in planners, productivity apps, sticky notes, wall calendars, habit trackers, and color-coded everything. From the outside, they look wildly organized. On the inside, they're still missing deadlines.

The issue usually isn't a lack of tools. It's too many tools.

Your system should make life easier, not become another full-time job.

KEEP IT SIMPLE, KEEP IT SINGLE

Pick:

- one main calendar for time-based commitments
- one main task list for to-dos

That's it.

You can use your phone calendar plus a notes app. You can use a paper planner. You can use a digital planning app if you genuinely like it. The key is: don't scatter your life across five places you never fully check.

If you love writing things by hand, you can still use a physical planner—just make sure big deadlines and appointments live in one master spot so nothing gets lost.

AUTOMATE THE OBVIOUS STUFF

Stop forcing your brain to remember things your phone can remember better.

Set recurring reminders for:

- bill due dates and rent
- regular assignments or quizzes
- weekly cleaning tasks
- club meetings or call-home nights
- birthdays and anniversaries

Automation isn't overkill; it's how you save brainpower for actual thinking instead of "Oh no, I forgot again."

MASTER THE BRAIN DUMP METHOD

When your mind is buzzing with fifty things at once, focusing on anything feels impossible.

That's when you do a brain dump:

1. Grab a notebook or notes app.
2. Write down *everything* swirling in your head: assignments, worries, texts you owe people, random "shoulds," errands, ideas.
3. Once it's all out, sort it: what's urgent, what's important, what can wait, what can be scheduled, what can be ignored.

Now your brain isn't trying to clutch 50 open tabs at once. You have a list. Lists are much less scary than vague mental chaos.

Marcus went through a phase where he kept downloading new productivity apps, convinced that *this one* would solve everything. Instead, his tasks ended up scattered between three different platforms, a whiteboard, and the back of his hand.

Deadlines slipped through the cracks because he didn't know where to look.

He finally deleted the extras and committed to his phone calendar and a single notes app. He set recurring reminders and used voice-to-text to capture tasks while walking between classes. Once he stopped babysitting five systems, he had energy left to actually do the work.

KEY TAKEAWAYS

College time management isn't about designing the "perfect" schedule. It's about:

- building a weekly rhythm that includes classes, work, rest, and life
- accepting that balance shifts week to week
- making *intentional* choices about where your energy goes
- Simple, consistent tools beat complicated systems you abandon after two days.

Your next moves -

- Track how you actually spend your time for three or four days.
- Build a basic weekly template: put in classes, work, and life maintenance first.
- Pick one calendar system and one main to-do list.
- Set recurring reminders for big, predictable things: rent, weekly chores, standing commitments.

With your time framework in place, the next step is learning how to communicate like a functioning adult—with professors, bosses, landlords, and everyone else who expects emails that sound like they came from a real person, not a panicked raccoon.

10

Emails, Phone Calls, and Grown-Up Communication

CRAFTING MESSAGES THAT OPEN DOORS

Cameron stared at his laptop screen for twenty minutes, typing and deleting the same email to his professor. He'd missed a deadline and needed an extension, but everything he wrote sounded either too casual or weirdly formal. He was hovering over "send" on version number seven when his roommate glanced over his shoulder and said, "Just be polite and direct. They're human too."

Professional email skills are one of those things everyone assumes you magically picked up somewhere, but most people learn through trial, error, and at least one cringe message they think about in the shower for years.

The goal is simple: respectful but human. You want to sound like a responsible adult, not a robot—or someone texting from the club at 1 AM.

Remember how we talked in the last chapter about managing your time like an adult instead of sprinting from crisis to crisis? Email is the communication version of that. Clear, thoughtful messages save you time, reduce stress, and make it way easier to get help, extensions, references, and opportunities… especially when you're emailing outside normal business hours.

GETTING THE TONE RIGHT

This is where most people trip up.

Too formal:

"Dear Sir or Madam, I humbly request your gracious consideration of my recent assignment..."

Too casual:

"hey lol so I kinda missed the deadline, can u reopen the portal??"

Aim for: polite, clear, and normal—like talking to someone older you respect, but don't know well yet.

Common tone mistakes to avoid:

• opening with "To Whom It May Concern" when you know their name

• turning the email into a whole life story when a paragraph would do

• using text abbreviations, all caps, or multiple exclamation marks

• demanding an instant response or acting like they owe you a favor

Emma learned this the embarrassing way when she sent a group email to her entire discussion section asking if anyone else thought the reading was "totally boring" – and forgot her professor was on the list.

Her follow-up email owned the mistake, apologized, and then actually engaged with the reading in a smarter way. Instead of tanking her reputation, it sparked a surprisingly good classroom conversation.

She realized professional communication isn't about being fake.

It's about being considerate of your audience and the context.

BEYOND EMAIL: PHONE CALLS AND FACE-TO-FACE

Sometimes, you actually have to talk to people. With your voice. In real time. Terrifying, but useful.

• Phone calls are better for urgent problems, confusing situations, or things that need back-and-forth questions.

• Face-to-face conversations (or video calls) are the gold standard for big topics: grades, recommendations, conflicts, or complicated personal situations.

These skills don't just matter with professors and campus offices. They become crucial in the next chapter when we dive into managing your health—because explaining symptoms clearly or sorting out insurance issues can literally affect your physical wellbeing.

Professional communication opens doors. Learn it now, and future you will quietly high-five past you every time an opportunity lands in your inbox instead of disappearing into the void.

MASTERING EVERY PHONE CALL ELEMENT

The phone rang in the financial aid office, and Ethan immediately felt his palms start to sweat. He'd been putting off calling about his student loan paperwork for weeks because he wasn't sure what to say—and because phone calls felt weirdly formal and stressful.

Then the automated voice launched into five different menu options. He almost hung up. Instead, he took a breath, grabbed a pen, and hit option 3 for financial aid.

Phone anxiety is real. But a lot of important "grown-up" things still happen over the phone: loans, housing, banking, healthcare, jobs. The trick is preparation and remembering: the person on the other end is literally paid to help you solve the problem.

PRE-CALL PREPARATION

Just like we planned your week in the last chapter, a good phone call starts *before* you dial. Have your stuff ready:

- account numbers, student ID, or reference codes
- pen and paper (or a notes app) for names and details
- your calendar if you might need to schedule something
- a semi-quiet spot where you won't be interrupted mid-call

Write one clear sentence about your goal for the call, like:

"I want to check why I was charged this fee and see if it can be reversed."

That way if you get transferred three times and your brain starts melting, you still remember why you called.

DURING THE CALL

Speak clearly. Don't rush. Bad connections and background noise mean people will just ask you to repeat yourself anyway.

Simple strategies that work:

- start with your name and reason for calling
- ask for their name and write it down
- request any case or reference numbers they create
- repeat back critical details ("So just to confirm...")
- ask them to slow down or repeat if you miss something

Lauren avoided calling her bank about a random fee until her balance was dangerously close to zero. When she finally called—with her account pulled up, a list of questions, and a notebook—she spent five minutes on the phone and the rep removed the charge on the spot.

She realized the dread was worse than the call. Now any time something looks off—fees, bills, financial aid confusion—she calls the same day instead of letting anxiety build for weeks.

VOICEMAIL MASTERY

Sometimes you get voicemail. Do **not** just hang up and hope they magically call back. Leave a message that's actually useful.

Include:

- your full name
- your phone number (said slowly)
- why you're calling (one sentence)
- best time to reach you
- your phone number again

Something like:

"Hi, this is Cameron Lee, C-A-M-E-R-O-N L-E-E. I'm a student calling about a question with my financial aid package. You can reach me at 555-123-4567. I'm usually free after 2 PM on weekdays. Again, that's 555-123-4567. Thanks."

SETTING YOURSELF UP FOR SUCCESS

These skills become essential when you're dealing with health clinics, insurance companies, and pharmacies—places where miscommunication gets expensive or risky fast.

The more you practice now—with office hours, financial aid, housing, campus jobs—the less terrifying phone calls feel later. Once you learn the pattern, it's just another adult skill you can pull out when needed.

DIGITAL BOUNDARIES THAT ACTUALLY WORK

The group chat in Sarah's shared apartment had turned into pure chaos.

In one endless scroll, you could find:

- memes
- someone's dating drama
- a reminder about the gas leak
- arguments about dishes
- three "who's buying toilet paper?" messages
- and a desperate "I have an exam tomorrow, please turn the music down" buried in the middle

When her roommate missed that exam message completely, Sarah realized they needed less chaos and more structure.

Digital communication feels casual, but it still *counts*. The way you use group chats, email, and messaging apps can either keep life smooth… or turn it into a constant stream of misunderstandings.

PLATFORM STRATEGY

Just like we organized your time into blocks, organize your communication by purpose. Rough guide:

- Text/WhatsApp/Group chat: quick plans, check-ins, casual stuff
- Email: anything important, official, or needing a record (landlords, professors, work, money)
- Slack/Teams/Group platforms: group projects, jobs, clubs
- Voice/video calls: urgent issues, emotional topics, complex conversations

Sarah's apartment now has two group chats:

• "Apartment Business" – for bills, chores, safety, schedules

• "Random Chaos" – for memes, TikToks, gossip, and nonsense

Nobody misses emergency or serious messages anymore. The gas leak doesn't get sandwiched between 20 GIFs.

DIGITAL TONE CONTROL

On-screen, you don't have facial expressions or tone of voice to soften what you say. That "lol" you think sounds friendly might land as sarcasm. That super short reply might read as annoyed, not busy.

Helpful habits:

• use full sentences for important messages

• add a bit of context when asking for something

• confirm you've seen key info ("Got it, thanks!")

• save sensitive or complicated topics for in-person or calls

• read your message once before sending and ask: "How would I read this if I were tired or stressed?"

Marcus learned about work chat the hard way when his manager texted, "Can you cover a shift Thursday?" and he replied, "yeah sure lol."

She later explained that while she appreciated the yes, the "lol" made it sound like he wasn't taking the job seriously. Now he treats work messages like mini emails: still short, but clear, respectful, and emoji-light.

RESPONSE TIME EXPECTATIONS

Not every message is an emergency. Life is easier when everyone has the same rough expectations for how fast people need to respond.

For example:

• Right away: real emergencies only (gas leak, safety issue, lost roommate)

• Same day: work stuff, academic deadlines, time-sensitive plans

• Within 24–48 hours: casual questions, "let's hang soon," longer discussions

• Whenever: memes, random thoughts, non-urgent group chat chaos

This matters even more when you're dealing with doctor portals, pharmacy messages, or insurance emails. Knowing what needs quick action and what doesn't keeps your brain calmer.

TURN TENSION INTO YOUR SUPERPOWER

Jessica knew she had to talk to her roommate about the bathroom situation. And by "situation," we mean: it was gross. He never cleaned it, and she was one toothpaste blob away from losing it.

Every time she thought about bringing it up, her heart raced and she imagined a defensive argument. She kept rehearsing the conversation in her head, and in every mental version he got offended and she ended up apologizing.

Finally, a friend suggested she write down what she wanted to say and treat it like a problem-solving conversation instead of a fight.

Difficult conversations feel scary, but avoiding them just lets the problem grow mold—sometimes literally.

STRATEGIC PREPARATION

Just like planning your week, tough conversations go better when you prep. Before you talk, get clear on:

- your main point in one sentence
- what you want to change
- what might be going on from their side
- one or two possible solutions

Aim for neutral, behavior-focused language, not personal attacks.

"The bathroom's been staying dirty and it's stressing me out" lands very differently from "You're disgusting."

TIMING AND ENVIRONMENT

Pick your moment.

- not five minutes before class
- not when someone's clearly exhausted or upset

• not in front of an audience

Private, calm, and un-rushed works best.

Jessica finally chose a quiet evening when they were both in the kitchen and said:

"Hey, can we talk about the bathroom for a minute? I've noticed it hasn't really been getting cleaned, and I'd love to figure out a system that works for both of us."

She framed it as a shared problem with a shared solution, not an attack. They ended up making a simple cleaning rotation and it stopped being a lingering resentment.

LANGUAGE THAT OPENS DOORS

Your words can make someone defensive... or open them up to problem-solving. A few tiny swaps help:

• "I've noticed..." instead of "You always..."

• "Can we figure out..." instead of "You need to..."

• "What if we tried..." instead of "You should..."

• "I get that you're busy, and..." instead of "You clearly don't care..."

Marcus had to talk to his boss about a shift that overlapped with a major exam. His first instinct was to lie and call in sick. Instead, he asked for a quick chat, explained the conflict honestly, and suggested swapping shifts or picking up an extra one later.

His manager appreciated the honesty and the proposed solution. They rearranged the schedule, his exam went fine, and he kept his job.

He realized: most people respond well to respectful honesty plus a plan.

MAKING IT WORK

These same communication muscles become critical in the next chapter when you're talking to doctors, nurses, and other health professionals. Being able to say, "Here's what's going on, here's what I need, here's what I'm worried about" clearly and calmly can change the care you receive.

Whether you're emailing a professor, texting your roommates, calling your bank, or explaining symptoms to a doctor, the core skills stay the same:

• prepare your main points

- choose the right channel and timing
- use clear, respectful language
- focus on solutions instead of blame

Communication gets easier every time you practice it. Every slightly awkward email you send, every phone call you survive, and every tough conversation you handle well is one more rep in the gym of adult life.

11

Health, Appointments, and Looking After Your Body

NAVIGATING YOUR HEALTH CARE PROVIDER CHOICES

Your body has officially come under new management: yours. That means knowing *where* to go when things hurt, itch, click, sting, or just feel… wrong. Most students can use the campus health center, but you also want a local primary care doctor in your corner for anything ongoing or anything that happens when campus is closed and you are not.

You can think about health care the same way you felt about communication tools in the last chapter. You would not use the same text for your crush, your landlord, and your grandma. Different situations, different channels. Same with medical care.

The campus health center is your low-effort, high-payoff option. It is usually near your classes, often covered by your student fees or offered at low cost, and it exists almost entirely for people living on caffeine and deadlines. You can see someone about a sore throat, talk through anxiety, get birth control, grab a vaccine, or sort out a prescription without Ubering across town.

The bonus is that they *get* students. They have seen stress rashes during finals, people who have forgotten what a vegetable looks like, and roommates sharing everything except sleep schedules. You do not have to explain why you have been awake since 2 a.m. for reasons that include both coursework and YouTube. They already assume it.

A local primary care doctor (or family doctor) is your longer-game partner. Campus health can handle the "I feel awful today" moments; your primary care doctor handles "this has been happening for months" and "I might need a specialist." If you have asthma, ADHD, diabetes, anxiety, or anything else that needs monitoring, your primary care doctor is the one keeping an eye on the bigger picture. They are also the person you turn to when you are still in your college town over summer break and the campus clinic is a ghost town.

Finding and choosing a primary care doctor near campus is a beginning-of-semester task, right alongside opening a bank account and figuring out which bus actually goes where you think it goes. You will need your insurance card, ID, and current address, which you have already had to wrangle for other grown-up tasks, so you should use that admin momentum.

Of course, life does not politely wait for office hours. That is where urgent care and walk-in clinics come in. They sit between "this can wait for a regular appointment" and "I probably need the ER." Think bad ear infections that show up on Sunday, mystery rashes after a hike, or a sprained ankle during a holiday when you are nowhere near campus or your usual doctor.

Urgent care clinics usually cost more than seeing the campus health center but less than an emergency room visit, especially once deductibles and copays are involved. They are the "I need help now but I am not dying" option.

Rose spent her whole first year winging it. No campus registration, no primary care doctor, just vibes and cough syrup. When she developed a cough that refused to leave for three weeks, she finally gave in and went to the campus health center. Registration took about five minutes. She got seen the same day. She left with an inhaler, real instructions, and a strong sense of regret that she had not done this during orientation week.

Save yourself Rose's story arc. Get set up with the campus health center and pick a primary care doctor while you still feel fine. Future you, who wakes up with strep throat the day before a presentation, will be very impressed.

MASTER THE ART OF APPOINTMENT BOOKING

Booking a medical appointment can feel like a boss battle: phone anxiety, confusing options, and a ticking clock while you try to remember your date of birth. Once you know what to say and what you need, it becomes just another adulting task you can absolutely handle.

Think of it like a short, professional version of those emails from the communication chapter. Same you, just with fewer emojis and more symptoms.

Before you contact the office, do a tiny bit of prep. Have your full name, date of birth, current address, and phone number ready. Keep your health insurance card in front of you and, if your school uses student IDs in their system, have that too. Jot down any regular meds you take and one or two clear sentences about what is going on.

You can keep all of this in your notes app so you are not trying to remember everything while the receptionist says, "Hi, how can I help you?" on repeat. The feeling is very similar to opening a spreadsheet you already set up: some past version of you has made today easier.

When it is time to describe your symptoms, vague is your enemy. "I feel weird" gives the receptionist nothing to work with. Saying that the problem started five days ago, is getting worse, keeps you awake, and is not responding to over-the-counter medicine helps them decide how soon you need to be seen and what kind of appointment to offer.

Your schedule is part of this puzzle too. Check your classes, work shifts, and club meetings before you call. Offices often have routine appointments booked weeks in advance, same-day slots for urgent things, and sometimes phone or video visits. If you can be flexible, you have more options. Early morning appointments often open up first. Slots squeezed between classes can work surprisingly well. For anything urgent, being willing to see whoever is available is usually more useful than waiting several days for your "preferred provider."

Nathan used to stare at his phone, rehearse what he wanted to say, then hang up as soon as he heard the hold music. His game changer was writing a mini script: his name, date of birth, a reminder that he was a patient there, and one sentence about his symptoms and how long they had been going on. Reading from the script made the whole call feel like following a recipe instead of improvising live on air.

If the idea of calling still makes your stomach flip, check the clinic's website. Many now let you request appointments, ask non-urgent questions, or request refills through an online portal. You might be able to sort everything out in three minutes from your laptop, no phone call required.

Once you conquer appointment booking, a lot of other adult admin starts to feel less scary. You have already proved you can talk to a stranger on the phone about something important, organize information, and fit it around your schedule. That same skill set works for job interviews, bank calls, and future "Hi, I am calling about that bill you sent me" moments.

TAKING CHARGE OF YOUR PRESCRIPTIONS

Medications are one of those areas where "my mom used to handle it" quietly stops working the minute you move out. Taking charge means knowing what you take, why you take it, and how to avoid the dreaded "I have one pill left and no refill" panic.

All those time management strategies from Chapter 9? They live here too. You are building little systems that keep you safe even when your brain is full of deadlines and group projects.

Refills are your best friend for anything long-term. Once you are set up for refills, you do not have to remember to request a new prescription every single month. Usually, you make sure your primary care doctor has your current medication list, choose a pharmacy you actually pass in real life, and request your refills a bit before you run out.

In many practices, prescriptions are sent electronically straight to your chosen pharmacy. Pharmacies often text you when your meds are ready. Some big chains let you order refills in their apps and will even mail your prescriptions to you, which feels like the most boring subscription box in the world and yet is absolutely lifesaving during finals week.

Then there is the "remembering to actually take it" part. Most medicines work best when you take them consistently, not just whenever you remember. That is especially true for things like inhalers, antidepressants, ADHD meds, and hormonal treatments.

You can use phone alarms, medication reminder apps, or old-school pill organizers that show you what you have already taken this week. Some people link meds to habits they never forget, like morning coffee, brushing their teeth, or their bedtime routine. The goal is to make taking your medication as automatic as opening your laptop in class.

Choosing a pharmacy near campus early on will pay off fast. Familiar staff recognize you, can answer questions about side effects in plain language, and can suggest over-the-counter options without you having to Google every symptom at 2 a.m. Look at their hours, whether they are on your usual route, and if they offer drive-through, pickup lockers, or delivery. Your future self walking home in the rain will appreciate a short detour instead of a cross-town trek.

Student discounts and loyalty programs on basic meds and health stuff are everywhere. The same stores selling your favorite snacks often have rewards programs on pain relievers, allergy meds, and vitamins. Using those deals is basically budgeting disguised as self-care.

Clara found out how much systems matter when she ran out of her anxiety meds right in the middle of exams. At home, her mom had always handled refills. At school, she suddenly realized she had no refills, no local pharmacy set up, and no extra pills. The new prescription took almost two weeks to sort out. It was a terrible time to be without the thing that helped keep her brain steady.

Now she has a reminder set for when she has about a week's supply left. She uses a pharmacy near campus during the semester and one near her family home during breaks. Whether she is cramming in the library or hanging out in her childhood bedroom, she can still pick up what she needs.

If you have any regular medication, build your own version of that system before you hit your own Clara moment. Keep a note on your phone with the names, doses, and the doctor who prescribed each one. Stick a paper copy somewhere in your room. If you ever end up in urgent care or the ER and need to explain what you take, that little list saves a lot of time and guesswork.

YOUR WELL-BEING TOOLKIT AND WARNING SIGNS

Health is not just "Do I have a diagnosis?" It is also "Can I stay awake in class?" "Do I cry every time I open my inbox?" and "When was the last time I ate something that was not beige?" Looking after yourself is about small habits that keep you at a level where life feels manageable, not heroic rescue missions every few months.

Sleep is the quiet engine behind all of it. When it works, lectures feel easier, people are less annoying, and you do not catch every cold on campus. When it does not, everything else feels heavier. Aim for something in the seven to nine-hour range most nights, not just once a week. Give your brain a little signal that bedtime is coming: closing the laptop, putting your phone out of reach, switching from intense study to something calmer.

Your room either helps or hurts here. A cooler, darker space makes falling asleep easier. In shared housing, earplugs, eye masks, and honest conversations about "please no blender at midnight" go a long way. Chapter 6 probably already convinced you that roommate agreements are not just for neat freaks.

Food and water are the other unglamorous heroes. Regular meals beat the binge-then-nothing pattern most student schedules encourage. Drinking water during the day keeps headaches and brain fog away more than people expect. Keeping a few easy options in your kitchen means you have something to eat that is not delivery when you drag yourself home after a late study session. That basic pasta or stir-fry from Chapter 7 really is doing more for your brain than you think.

Mental health needs check-ins too. Everyone has stressful weeks; that is part of the deal. The trick is noticing when "busy and a bit frazzled" turns into "I feel like this all the time." Changes that last more than a couple of weeks matter: sleep going off the rails, losing interest in stuff you usually enjoy, feeling permanently overwhelmed by your to-do list, zoning out in lectures, or snapping at people constantly.

Marcus spent months insisting he was "just not a morning person." In reality, he was scrolling until 3 a.m., waking up wrecked, and then dragging himself through 9 a.m. classes like a zombie. When he started leaving his phone in another room at 11 p.m. and aiming for a midnight bedtime, his mornings improved within days. He did not need a whole personality change; he needed a charger that was not right next to his pillow.

Taking charge of your health does not mean diagnosing yourself online or becoming an expert in every condition. It means knowing roughly how the system works, paying attention to your own patterns, and asking for help sooner rather than later.

Sign up with the campus health center and choose a primary care doctor before you are desperate for an appointment. Practice booking visits until it feels like just another admin task. Set up prescription routines that do not rely on anyone else remembering for you. Check in with your sleep, your food, and your mood the way you check your bank balance.

Once those basics are in place, you are ready for the next step: staying safe in the wider world outside campus, classes, and your room. That is where we are heading next.

12

Personal Safety - On Campus, Nights Out, and Travel

YOUR SAFE JOURNEY HOME STRATEGY

It's 2 AM, you're leaving a party across town, and your original ride just texted, "Sorry, had to go." Your phone battery is at 15%, you're not entirely sure where you are, and walking home alone feels… dicey.

This kind of scenario happens more often than people admit. A plan you make *before* you go out is what stops "fun night" from turning into "terrifying story you tell your therapist later."

BEFORE YOU LEAVE HOME

Plan your way home *before* you lock the door behind you. Have more than one option lined up:

- a designated driver
- at least one rideshare app you know how to use
- bus or train times saved
- a reliable friend you can call if everything else falls apart

Keep some emergency cash tucked in your wallet or phone case. Apps glitch, cards get declined, and Wi-Fi disappears right when you need it. A $20 bill can be the difference between getting home safely and trying to "figure it out" at 3 AM in an unfamiliar neighborhood.

Download more than one rideshare app so you're not stuck with surge pricing or zero drivers. Check the last bus or train times for your area and screenshot them. When you're tired, tipsy, or stressed, your brain will not want to load another transit website.

COMMUNICATION IS YOUR SAFETY NET

Location sharing isn't just for nosy parents; it's a safety tool.

Share your location with one or two trusted friends and tell someone when you expect to be home. Most phones and messaging apps let you share your live location for a set time.

Text a roommate or close friend when you leave:

"Heading back from Jake's, Uber ETA 15 mins. I should be home by 2:10."

If something delays you, they'll notice and check in.

REAL-WORLD EXAMPLE

Andrew learned this the hard way when his designated driver left the party with someone else and stopped answering messages. His phone died, he had no cash, and he ended up walking two miles through a sketchy area at 3 AM, passing groups of people who made him seriously uncomfortable.

Now he always:

- carries twenty dollars in cash
- keeps a portable charger in his bag
- has multiple rideshare apps installed
- texts his roommate when he heads home

Nothing dramatic has happened since—but that's exactly the point.

TRUST YOUR GUT

If something feels off about a ride or route, pay attention to that feeling.

- the driver smells like alcohol
- the car doesn't match the app
- the route feels wrong and you're suddenly "taking a short-cut" through a dark area

Get out of the situation. Cancel the ride, ask to get dropped in a well-lit public spot, or call someone else. Your safety is more valuable than an awkward moment or a cancelation fee.

Taking care of your health isn't just about clinics and checkups. It includes avoiding situations where your body or safety is at risk in the first place.

NAVIGATING SOCIAL SPACES WITH CARE

You see your friend Violet at a crowded bar. Something feels off. She looks way more out of it than two drinks should explain, and the person she's talking to keeps leaning in and trying to steer her away from your group.

These are the moments when you decide whether to stay "polite" or step in. This is where having a plan with your friends pays off.

THE BUDDY SYSTEM WORKS

Make a simple agreement with your group before you go out:

- no one leaves alone
- if someone wants to leave with a new person, they check in with the group first
- at least one person stays relatively sober and keeps an eye on things

This isn't about controlling anyone. It's a safety net for those moments when judgment is foggy or someone feels pressured.

Have a quick pre-night-out chat:

- What's our meet-up point if we get separated?
- Who's the least likely to be drinking heavily tonight?
- How will we handle someone wanting to leave with a stranger?

The first time you bring it up it might feel awkward. After that, it just becomes "how our group does things."

RECOGNIZING WARNING SIGNS

Learn the classic signs of a spiked drink or someone who's more impaired than makes sense for what they've had:

- sudden dizziness or confusion
- feeling extremely drunk after one or two drinks
- slurred speech that comes on fast
- trouble standing or walking

• gaps in memory or not understanding where they are

Other red flags:

• someone ignoring boundaries or "no"

• a person trying to isolate your friend from the group

• pressure to keep drinking when your friend clearly wants to stop

All those communication skills from earlier chapters matter here. Being direct and firm can stop a bad situation before it escalates.

CODE WORDS AND EXIT STRATEGIES

Create simple code phrases or signals that mean "I need help" or "Get me out of here."

It can be as basic as:

• "Can you come to the bathroom with me?"

• "I need water, can you help me?"

• or a specific emoji in the group chat

The point is: you can ask for backup without announcing it to the entire room.

REAL-WORLD APPLICATION

Violet and her roommates use a system in their group chat:

• if anyone texts "call me now," someone immediately calls with a fake emergency that requires them to leave

• if someone sends a specific emoji, it means "come stand next to me now"

They've used it twice:

• once when a guy wouldn't take no for an answer

• once when a friend felt strangely unsteady after one drink

Both times, the group stepped in, and they left together. Nothing "dramatic" happened—and that's the win.

Protecting your physical and mental health includes staying safe in social spaces. Knowing when to step in for yourself or someone else is a core adult skill.

Never apologize for choosing safety over social smoothness.

SPOTTING TROUBLE BEFORE IT FINDS YOU

The party seemed chill when you arrived. Two hours later, there's shouting in the kitchen, someone is passing around pills, and you realize you don't actually know anyone here except the one friend who invited you—and they've vanished.

This is the moment your instincts start whispering, "We should leave." Your job is to listen before they have to start screaming.

READING THE ROOM

Your nervous system notices shifts before your brain catches up:

- the vibe goes from relaxed to tense
- people start yelling or slamming doors
- drinks are flowing fast and nobody seems in control
- people are talking about drugs or illegal stuff like it's no big deal

When things start escalating, don't wait to see "how it plays out." It's easier to leave early than to extract yourself once things explode.

STAYING IN SAFE ZONES

Stick to well-lit, populated spaces, especially if you're not with people you trust.

- avoid back rooms, basements, or isolated corners when you're with strangers
- if someone keeps trying to get you alone, pause and ask why
- keep your phone charged and on you

Your exit plan is part of your safety plan. The ride apps, cash, and backup options from earlier in this chapter matter here too.

PROTECTING YOURSELF FROM SUBSTANCES

Basic rules that save a lot of grief:

- only accept drinks you see poured or open them yourself
- keep your drink in your hand or where you can see it

- if a drink tastes off, stop drinking it
- never let anyone pressure you into taking something you don't recognize or don't want

Pressure to "just chill" or "stop being dramatic" is its own red flag. People who care about you respect your limits.

LEARNING FROM EXPERIENCE

Ian went to a house party off campus. Pretty quickly he noticed:

- the hosts were pushing heavy drinking
- some guests seemed much older than college age
- people were hinting about "after-party plans" that made him uncomfortable

Instead of shrugging it off, he found his friends and said, "I'm not feeling good about this place. Can we bounce?" They all left together.

Later, they heard the party got broken up by police and several people were arrested. Leaving early saved them a lot of trouble—and possibly worse.

Listening to your gut isn't "overreacting." It's self-protection.

YOUR CAMPUS SAFETY TOOLKIT ESSENTIALS

One night, Susan was walking back to her dorm after a late study session. A man started walking behind her, matching her pace turn for turn. Her hands were shaking too much to dial 911 accurately, but she managed to open her campus safety app and hit the emergency button.

The app sent her location to campus security and her emergency contacts. A security officer met her within minutes and walked her back to her building. She got home safe because she'd set up her tools ahead of time.

ESSENTIAL DIGITAL TOOLS

Set up your safety tech on a calm afternoon, not in the middle of a panic. Useful tools include:

- your school's campus safety app (many have: emergency call, virtual escort, mass alerts)

• built-in phone safety features (emergency SOS, medical ID, location sharing)

• at least one friend who can see your location when you're out at night

Program important numbers into your contacts:

• campus security
• local police non-emergency line
• trusted roommates or friends
• family emergency contact

Practice pulling them up quickly, even with one hand, even when you're nervous.

KNOW YOUR RESOURCES

Take a daytime walk around campus with your safety brain turned on:

• where are the blue-light or emergency call boxes?
• which buildings stay open late?
• where is the campus police or security office?
• which routes feel the safest at night?

Many campuses offer:

• security escort services after dark
• late-night shuttle buses
• 24-hour study spaces you can duck into if you feel unsafe

These are only useful if you already know they exist and how to reach them.

BUILDING YOUR SAFETY NETWORK

After a close call walking alone, Austin sat down and built a safety setup:

• downloaded his university's safety app
• added campus security and local non-emergency police to his contacts
• signed up for text alerts from campus
• learned how to request a security escort
• shared locations with his roommate for late-night walks

Later, when a friend messaged him during a campus security alert, he already knew who to call and what to do.

RECAP OF KEY POINTS

Personal safety is not about constant fear. It's about:

- planning your way home before you go out
- looking out for your friends and letting them look out for you
- trusting your instincts when something feels off
- using tech and campus resources to back up your decisions

Most scary situations never happen when you prepare well, leave early when the vibe turns bad, and choose safety over trying to please strangers.

ACTION STEPS

This week, take an hour and:

- download your campus safety app and test the non-emergency features
- save emergency numbers in your phone
- set up location sharing with one or two trusted people
- talk with your friends about ride plans, buddy systems, and code words
- pick your "default" safe routes to and from the places you go most

Your physical safety is one half of modern self-protection. The other half lives on your phone, laptop, and social media. Next, you'll build the same kind of safety net for your digital life—protecting your money, your identity, and your future reputation online.

13

Digital Life & Online Safety in the Modern World

LOCK DOWN YOUR DIGITAL LIFE

Your digital life is basically your whole life now: banking, uni accounts, socials, shopping, streaming, and work stuff all live behind a login screen. A weak password is like leaving your front door wide open with a neon sign that says "Expensive things inside."

Strong passwords and two-factor authentication are the boring heroes that quietly stop identity theft, drained bank accounts, and "surprise" logins to your university portal at 3 AM from another country.

Think about one ordinary day online. You:

- check your bank balance
- log into your university portal
- open your email
- scroll social media
- order something online
- maybe access work or internship systems

Every single login is a potential doorway for someone who wants your money, your data, or your identity. The good news: you don't need to be a tech genius to shut most of those doors.

PASSWORD BASICS THAT ACTUALLY WORK

Treat important accounts like VIP sections: they each need their own password and it can't be the same "one good password" used everywhere.

Use unique, complex passwords for:

- banking and payment apps
- university email and portal
- major social media accounts
- your main cloud storage (Google Drive, iCloud, etc.)

When one website gets hacked and leaks your password, scammers immediately try that same login on banking sites, email, and anything else they can find. This is called "credential stuffing," and it works disturbingly often.

A password manager makes this manageable. Tools like Bitwarden, 1Password, or LastPass:

- generate long, random passwords for every site
- store them in an encrypted vault
- auto-fill them for you

You only remember one strong master password; the app remembers everything else. Many colleges give students free or discounted access to password managers through campus IT, so it's worth checking.

Avoid using personal info in passwords. Birthdays, pet names, sports teams, favorite bands, and hometowns are easy to find on social media.

Bad examples:

- Liverpool2023!
- Jessica1995
- 12345678
- password

Better examples:

- Kf9$mPx2@nQ7
- Purple#House92*Moon
- 8xR@film$Tree3

They look ridiculous on purpose. That's exactly why they're safer.

TWO-FACTOR AUTHENTICATION IS YOUR SAFETY NET

Two-factor authentication (2FA) adds one extra step between "someone has my password" and "someone is sitting inside my account."

With 2FA turned on, logging in usually needs:

1 your password

2 a code from your phone (text or app) or a physical security key

Even if your password leaks, the code changes every 30 seconds, which makes accounts dramatically harder to break into.

Wherever you see "enable two-factor authentication" or "multi-factor authentication," turn it on for:

- email
- banking and cash apps
- university accounts
- social media
- password manager

Use an authenticator app like Google Authenticator, Microsoft Authenticator, or Authy when you can. Text-message codes are better than nothing, but texts can be intercepted or SIM-swapped. Authenticator apps live on your phone and generate codes locally, which is harder to mess with.

William thought his password "Liverpool2023!" was genius until he got locked out of his university email. Someone guessed it, changed his recovery settings, and tried to reroute his financial aid notifications. It took three days and several calls to IT support to fix. His Instagram was basically a giant hint about his password: Liverpool merch, game photos, and "YNWA" captions everywhere.

Once he switched to a password manager and turned on 2FA, the drama stopped.

These habits don't just protect your college accounts. They're the same skills you'll need when you're dealing with payroll systems, client data, and work email later.

SPOTTING DIGITAL DECEPTION BEFORE IT STRIKES

Scammers love students. You're juggling classes, money stress, financial aid forms, and fifty different logins. That mix of pressure and inexperience is exactly what they're counting on.

The tactics are the same ones we talked about in real-world safety: create panic, rush you, and hope you react before you think. The difference is that online they can reach you at 7 AM, midnight, or during your 3-minute break between classes.

COMMON STUDENT-TARGETED SCAMS

You'll see versions of these again and again:

• Fake financial aid alerts

"Your FAFSA has been suspended" or "Your student loan payment is overdue, click here to avoid collections." Real federal student loan services (ending in .gov) do not text you surprise panic links.

• Phishing emails pretending to be your university, bank, or Netflix

They say things like "verify your account" or "update payment details" and link to a fake login page that steals your credentials. Logos and formatting often look almost perfect.

• Scholarship scams

"Guaranteed scholarship, only $49 to apply." Any "scholarship" that asks for an application fee is basically charging you for nothing. Legit scholarships do not require payment just to submit.

• Romance scams

Someone on a dating app or social media moves very fast emotionally, then suddenly needs money for an "emergency," travel ticket, or medical bill. They use emotional pressure so you feel cruel if you say no.

RED FLAGS THAT SCREAM "SCAM"

Slow down when you see:

- extreme urgency: "respond in 10 minutes or your account is closed"
- threats: "you will be arrested / sued / reported immediately"
- unexpected money: "you've won a prize you never entered for"
- payment requests via gift cards, crypto, or wire transfers
- weird grammar, odd capitalization, or strange phrasing

Legitimate institutions rarely communicate like that, and they never demand payment in Amazon gift cards.

HOW TO VERIFY BEFORE YOU TRUST

A few habits stop most scams in their tracks:

- Inspect the sender address, not just the display name

"Chase Bank" support@chaselogins-help.com is not Chase. Watch for extra words, wrong endings (.co instead of .com or .gov), or misspellings.

- Ignore the link, go to the source yourself

Don't click. Open a new tab, type the official site (like irs.gov, studentaid.gov, your bank's real domain), and log in that way. Or call the number on the back of your card.

- Ask a human you trust

Show the message to a roommate, friend, or family member: "Does this look legit to you?"

Scammers rely on you feeling embarrassed or rushed. A second pair of eyes often spots the nonsense instantly.

Stella got a text saying her student loan account was "suspended" and she had to "verify immediately" via a link. Her heart rate spiked, because losing financial aid was her worst nightmare. Then she noticed the sender name looked off and the link was a sketchy URL instead of a .gov address. She closed it, went directly to the official loan site, and called their support line. They confirmed everything on her account was fine and that the message was a scam designed to capture login and bank details.

Calm checking beat panic tapping.

Staying on top of your budget and bank accounts (remember

Chapter 2) makes it easier to catch small weird charges early, before they turn into full-blown fraud.

YOUR DIGITAL FOOTPRINT SURVIVAL GUIDE

Your social media is basically your public shop window. Future employers, internship supervisors, landlords, scholarship committees, and dates will look you up long before you know they exist.

The version of you that lives online doesn't automatically update when you grow up. That rant you posted at 17, the party photos, the "jokes" about hating work—those can show up years later.

THE REALITY CHECK

That photo of you passed out on someone's floor might be hilarious to your friends. The hiring manager for your dream internship will not find it as charming.

Posts trashing teachers, bosses, coworkers, or classmates make you look unreliable and hard to work with. Screenshots travel, even from "private" spaces.

Even simple things like who you follow, what you like, and the comments you leave under posts build a picture of you.

PRIVACY SETTINGS ARE YOUR BEST FRIEND

Once a semester, do a quick privacy tune-up:

- check who can see your posts, stories, and tagged photos
- limit location sharing to trusted friends
- review old albums and decide what still needs to exist

Most platforms quietly change features over time. A setting you chose freshman year might not mean the same thing now.

Also check "tag review" options that let you approve photos before they appear on your profile. Friends might have a very different idea of what counts as "fine to post."

THE PROFESSIONAL TEST

Before you post, ask:

"Would I be okay with a future boss seeing this on a giant screen behind me during a job interview?"

If the answer is even a shaky "uhhh… maybe not," reconsider. That applies to:

• photos
• memes
• comment threads
• usernames

Consider running separate spaces:

• a professional LinkedIn with your real name, photo, and achievements
• a more private Instagram or TikTok locked down to friends

Your future self will thank you for this separation.

CLEANUP TIME

Spend one afternoon doing a digital spring clean:

1 Google your name plus your school and city.
2 Check image results as well as web pages.
3 Delete or hide old posts that no longer match who you are.
4 Untag yourself from chaotic party pics.
5 Update cringey usernames and bios.

Marcus nailed his interview for a local restaurant job, then never heard back. A friend later told him the manager saw his public Instagram filled with posts bragging about skipping shifts at a different job, getting wasted, and calling customers "the worst." His online persona completely contradicted the responsible worker he presented in person.

He spent an afternoon cleaning up, turned his account private, and created a more professional presence for future applications.

Your online self can either quietly sabotage you or quietly support you.

YOUR DIGITAL FOOTPRINT UNDER THE MICROSCOPE

Your digital footprint doesn't disappear after graduation. Employers, grad schools, landlords, and sometimes even disciplinary boards use online searches as part of their decision-making.

This isn't about becoming a fake, polished robot. It's about choosing what you put on the public stage instead of leaving your reputation to chance.

MONITOR YOUR DIGITAL PRESENCE

Every couple of months, do a quick audit:

• google your name and scroll a few pages in

• try different versions: nickname + last name, full name + university, name + hometown

• check Google Images too

You can also set up Google Alerts for your name so you get an email if something new appears. If your name is common, add your school or field.

CREATE POSITIVE CONTENT

The best way to push down old or random search results is to create better ones.

Ideas:

• a solid LinkedIn profile with your photo, major, and experience

• a simple personal site or portfolio page (even a basic "about me + projects" setup)

• posts about internships, volunteering, projects, and interests in your field

Share articles related to what you're studying and add a short comment: what you found interesting, what you agree or disagree with, or how it connects to your classes.

Thoughtful content shows you can think, not just scroll.

MANAGE WHAT OTHERS SHARE

Talk with close friends about your goals:

"I'm applying for internships soon, can we cool it on tagging me in blackout photos?"

Turn on tag approval where possible, and don't be afraid to untag yourself or ask for something to be taken down. Most friends will understand once you explain why.

Remember: even in group photos, you're recognizable. You don't need a tag for someone to say "Oh, that's them."

Ava's career advisor casually said, "Have you googled yourself lately?" She had not. What she found:

- party photos where she looked extremely drunk
- old tweets complaining about professors
- jokes that felt funny at 16 and awful at 21

She spent a weekend:

- untagging herself from the worst photos
- deleting old tweets
- tightening privacy settings
- building a basic LinkedIn with her major, GPA, and volunteer work

When she landed her dream internship, her supervisor later mentioned they were impressed by how professional she seemed online. The messy content they *would* have seen simply did not exist anymore.

YOUR DIGITAL LIFE SUMMARY

Your online world is plugged directly into your real-world future:

- strong, unique passwords and 2FA keep strangers out of your accounts
- scam awareness protects your money, identity, and sanity
- intentional social media use keeps your future options wide open
- a managed digital footprint helps opportunities find you instead of quietly closing doors

TAKE ACTION NOW

Pick a day this week and:

- install a password manager and change passwords on your most important accounts
- turn on two-factor authentication everywhere that offers it
- review privacy settings on your main social apps

• google yourself and clean up anything that no longer fits who you are

• create or update a basic LinkedIn profile, even if you're only a first-year

You've just built the digital version of locking your front door, clearing your front yard, and putting your best self in the window.

Next up, you'll shift from protecting your future to actively building it: networking, jobs, internships, and the professional life that all this groundwork has been quietly preparing you for.

14

Part-Time Jobs, Internships, and Professional Basics

LANDING YOUR PERFECT STUDENT JOB

When Caleb started college, his parents had always handled everything—from booking his dentist appointments to calling restaurants for reservations. The idea of actually applying for jobs felt... like a boss level he'd skipped all the tutorials for. After scrolling through endless job listings that all seemed to require three years of experience and seventeen skills he didn't have, he almost gave up.

Then his roommate casually mentioned that the campus library was hiring. No huge online posting, no scary application portal—just a "Help Wanted" sign and a friendly manager. That's when Caleb realized he'd been looking in all the wrong places.

The secret to finding a good student job?

It's not magic. It's knowing where to look and what employers actually want from students.

Most student jobs are not hiding on giant national job sites. They're:

- Tucked away on campus job boards
- Sitting quietly in local businesses near campus
- Shared through professors, friends, and group chats

CAMPUS-BASED JOBS: YOUR EASIEST STARTING POINT

Campus employers *get* student life. They know you have midterms, finals, group projects, and surprise labs that eat your soul.

Common on-campus jobs include:

- Library assistants and circulation desk staff
- Student union and front desk workers
- Dining hall, coffee cart, or café workers
- Campus tour guides and orientation leaders
- Research assistants and departmental office helpers
- Gym front desk staff, equipment checkout, rec center jobs
- Computer lab monitors and tech help desks

These jobs usually:

- Work around your class schedule
- Understand finals week is a war zone
- Sometimes let you study during slower shifts (the holy grail)

LOCAL BUSINESSES NEAR CAMPUS

Walkable distance from campus is where you'll find businesses that basically run on student workers. Think:

- Coffee shops and fast-casual restaurants
- Retail stores and bookstores
- Tutoring centers and test-prep companies
- Movie theaters, bowling alleys, mini-golf, escape rooms
- Campus-adjacent bars and event venues (if you're old enough, obviously)

They've usually hired students for years, which means they:

- Expect semester-based availability
- May offer more hours than campus jobs
- Sometimes have perks like free food, discounts, or chill late-night shifts

SEASONAL AND GIG WORK: MONEY WITHOUT LONG-TERM COMMITMENT

If your semester is already intense, or you only want to work sometimes, seasonal and gig jobs can be perfect:

- Holiday retail work (November–January rush)

• Summer camp counselor or summer school aide
• Event staffing for concerts, sports games, or conferences
• Food delivery and rideshare (if you have a car and meet age requirements)
• Freelance tutoring (high schoolers, SAT/ACT, specific subjects)
• Pet-sitting, dog walking, or housesitting

Lauren assumed the "good" jobs would appear in some magical listing online. But her favorite job came from simply walking into the campus bookstore on a slow afternoon and saying, "Hey, are you hiring?"

The manager said, "We don't have a posting up yet, but actually... yes."

She got the job before it ever hit the website.

Sometimes the best opportunities go to the people who show up and ask, not just the ones clicking "Apply."

Remember those professional communication skills from Chapter 10? A short, polite email or a confident, friendly in-person conversation ("Hi, I'm a student here and I'm wondering if you're hiring") can move you to the front of the line—especially when others are hiding behind generic online applications.

And don't forget your digital safety skills from Chapter 13:

• Research employers before sending personal info
• Be skeptical of "work from home, make $1,000 a day, no experience needed" jobs
• Never pay money to "get hired"

The right student job sits in the sweet spot:

decent pay + flexible hours + useful experience.

It exists—you just need to know where to look and how to present yourself when you find it.

RESUME SECRETS THAT LAND INTERVIEWS

Marcus spent three days crafting what he thought was a masterpiece resume. It included:

• An "objective statement" about "leveraging synergistic opportunities"
• Three bullet points about his high school chess club presidency
• A font so tiny you needed a microscope to read it

Two weeks and zero responses later, he realized he'd made the classic student mistake: trying to sound impressive instead of clear and relevant.

Your first resume doesn't have to scream "future CEO."

It just needs to say:

"I'm reliable. I'm not a chaos gremlin. I can learn stuff. You can trust me with your customers and your cash drawer."

THE ONLY SECTIONS YOU ACTUALLY NEED

Keep it to **one page** and focus on:

Contact info

◦ Name

◦ Phone

◦ Professional email (e.g., firstname.lastname@...)

Education

◦ Your college

◦ Major (if declared)

◦ Expected graduation year

◦ Relevant coursework if it fits the job (e.g., "Intro to Accounting" for a bookkeeping role)

Experience

◦ Any paid work

◦ Babysitting, tutoring, lifeguarding, yard work, etc.

◦ Volunteer roles and leadership in clubs

Skills

◦ Languages

◦ Software (Google Suite, Excel, Canva, etc.)

◦ Certifications (CPR, food handling, first aid)

Availability

◦ Which days/times you can usually work

You don't need:

- An "objective statement"
- "References available upon request" (everyone knows)
- A life story starting in 9th grade

MAKE TINY EXPERIENCES SOUND LIKE REAL RESPONSIBILITIES

Instead of vague fluff:

- ❌ "Helped customers"
- ✅ "Assisted 20+ customers per shift with questions and purchases"
- ❌ "Babysat kids"
- ✅ "Provided evening childcare for 2–3 children ages 3–10, including homework help, meals, and bedtime"
- ❌ "Volunteer"
- ✅ "Volunteered 3 hours weekly organizing donations and stocking shelves at local food pantry"

Numbers and specifics make even small roles feel professional.

FORMATTING: DON'T GET CUTE

Employers look at your resume for maybe 10–30 seconds. Make it painless:

- Simple, readable font (Arial, Calibri, Times New Roman)
- Clear headings and bullet points
- Consistent formatting (dates, job titles, spacing)
- Save and send as a PDF, not a Word doc that might break on their computer

Proofread like your grade depends on it. Then ask a friend, RA, or career center to proofread again.

COVER LETTERS THAT DON'T SUCK

A cover letter is just a short note that says:

1 Why you're interested in them

2 Why you'd be useful to them

3 That you're available and eager to learn

Structure:

- Paragraph 1:

"I'm a first-year [major] student, and I'd love to work at [place] because…"

- Paragraph 2:

"I have experience with [customer service / kids / fast-paced environments] from [job/volunteering], where I…"

• Paragraph 3:

"I'm available [days/times], and I'd be excited to learn more about the role."

Emma was embarrassed that her only "job" was babysitting. But on her resume it became:

"Childcare provider responsible for safety, meals, and activities for children ages 3–10."

In her cover letter, she added that she wanted to work at that specific coffee shop because she liked their atmosphere and values, and she mentioned their community events by name.

The manager later told her: it wasn't her experience that impressed him most—it was that she clearly cared enough to learn about the place and tailor her application.

CLASSIC STUDENT RESUME MISTAKES TO DODGE

• Using an email like partygirl2024@... or stonerlegend@...

• Listing every high school club you joined for three weeks sophomore year

• Claiming skills you don't have ("fluent in Excel" but you can only bold text)

• Turning a simple resume into a two-page manifesto

• Sending the exact same resume to every job without tweaking it

Think back to your budget from Chapter 2. You had to decide what was essential and what was "nice but not necessary." Do the same with your resume content.

Also: don't put your Social Security number, full home address, or other sensitive info on your resume. City and state are enough. Your digital safety rules from Chapter 13 still apply.

The goal isn't a perfect resume. It's a clear, honest one that gets you into the interview, where your actual personality, reliability, and enthusiasm can do the rest.

MASTERING YOUR PROFESSIONAL GAME PLAN

On Derek's third day working in the campus dining hall, the walk-in freezer died. No supervisor in sight. No instructions. Just beeping alarms and rising panic.

He thought, "Should I just ignore it? Try to fix it? Pretend I saw nothing?"

Instead, he remembered the "Contacts in an emergency" list by the phone, called the main office, explained the situation, and followed their instructions.

Later, his supervisor thanked him for handling it exactly right. Not because he fixed the freezer himself, but because he communicated and didn't just freeze (pun absolutely intended).

Professionalism isn't about never messing up.

It's about:

- showing up
- communicating clearly
- taking responsibility
- learning from mistakes

PUNCTUALITY: THE LOWEST-HANGING PROFESSIONAL FRUIT

You don't need special skills to:

- Show up 5–10 minutes early for shifts
- Check your schedule in advance
- Set alarms and calendar reminders
- Plan your commute with buffer time

If you're going to be late for real reasons (bus broke down, emergency, sudden illness):

- Call (not text if possible)
- Give them an ETA
- Apologize briefly—no dramatic overshare required

Sarah once showed up 20 minutes late to her retail shift and just quietly slipped in, hoping nobody noticed. Her manager did notice—and was more irritated that she hadn't called than about the lateness itself.

A quick call like, "Hey, the bus is stuck in traffic, I'm running about 15 minutes behind, I'm really sorry," would've gone a long way.

COMMUNICATION FUNDAMENTALS AT WORK

Those communication skills from Chapter 10? This is where they shine.

Good workplace communication means you:

- Ask when you're not sure instead of guessing
- Confirm important details ("Just to confirm, you want me to close at 9 and set the alarm?")
- Let your supervisor know when you've finished a task and what's next
- Keep them informed if something's going wrong

BE THE "SOLUTIONS, NOT JUST PROBLEMS" PERSON

Compare these two:

- ❌ "The printer's broken."
- ✅ "The printer's jammed. I tried clearing it using the instructions on the front, but it's still stuck. Do you want me to call IT or use the backup printer?"

The second one says: "I noticed a problem, I tried something reasonable, and I'm asking what you want next." That's gold to supervisors.

BUILDING YOUR PROFESSIONAL REPUTATION (WITHOUT BEING FAKE)

You don't need to be hyper-formal or painfully cheerful. Instead, aim for:

- Learning people's names and using them
- Offering help when you're not busy
- Taking feedback without getting defensive
- Being willing to learn new tasks

Managing your work-study balance is part of professionalism too:

- Don't do homework in front of customers
- Don't scroll your phone every five seconds
- Don't "forget" to mention exam week until the last minute
- Do share busy weeks in advance so schedules can be adjusted

These jobs are practice rounds for your future career. The habits you build now—showing up on time, communicating clearly, solving problems—will make internships and full-time jobs so much easier later.

JUGGLING CAREER DEMANDS AND LIFE'S PRIORITIES

Sophie was thrilled when she landed a well-paying restaurant job. Great tips, fun coworkers, free food—10/10.

Three weeks later, she was:

- working 25 hours a week
- taking a full load of classes
- falling asleep in lectures
- turning in assignments late

Her bank account looked healthier. Her brain did not.

She realized something important:

A job that wrecks your grades and health is not actually a good deal.

KNOW YOUR REAL LIMITS (NOT YOUR FANTASY ONES)

Most full-time students do best around 10–15 hours per week of work. Some can manage 20. Some are maxed out at 8. It depends on:

- your major (engineering vs. one writing-heavy class and vibes)
- your commute time
- your sleep needs
- mental/physical health
- other commitments (sports, clubs, family responsibilities)

Use your time management work from Chapter 9:

- Map out class hours
- Add study time (at least 2–3 hours per credit per week, in an ideal world)
- Add commuting, meals, basic life tasks
- See what's left over before you fill every gap with work

COMMUNICATING WITH EMPLOYERS LIKE AN ADULT

Most managers are not evil overlords trying to ruin your GPA. But they are not psychic either.

Be upfront from the start:

• "I'm a full-time student, and I'm looking for about 10–15 hours a week."

• "I can't work Tuesday and Thursday evenings because of labs, but I'm open all day Saturday."

Once you're hired:

• Ask for consistent shifts when possible—it makes planning easier

• Give early notice for exams or major projects

• Offer compromises:

"I've got two big exams that week. Could I drop one shift that week if I pick up an extra next week?"

Marcus thought asking for reduced hours during finals would make him look lazy. Instead, when he gave his manager two weeks' notice and offered to help cover more shifts afterward, his manager appreciated the maturity and kept him in mind for future leadership roles.

Honest communication builds trust.

WORK EXPERIENCE = FUTURE REFERENCES

Every supervisor, shift lead, and coworker is a potential:

• LinkedIn connection

• reference for internships

• job contact years later

To turn student jobs into future opportunities:

• Show up consistently

• Do your job without constant reminders

• Let supervisors see you handle responsibility

• Ask for feedback occasionally ("Is there anything I could be doing better?")

Check in with your digital footprint from Chapter 13 too—if you're connected with supervisors on social media, make sure your public persona doesn't scream "I hate working" or "I'm always drunk."

MONEY VS. TIME: DOING THE REAL MATH

Your budgeting skills from Chapter 2 come back here. Ask yourself:

- How much do I actually *need* to earn to cover my essentials?
- Is working extra hours now worth the hit to my grades and stress level?
- Will a lower GPA cost me more in the long term than I'm making in extra shifts?

Sometimes saying no to more hours is actually the financially smart move long-term—especially if it protects scholarships, keeps you on track to graduate, or leaves you time to pursue internships that matter for your career.

RED FLAGS IN STUDENT JOBS

Watch out if:

- You're constantly exhausted, sick, or on the edge of tears
- Your grades are sliding and you never have time to catch up
- You never see friends or take breaks
- Your employer refuses to work around exams or your class schedule
- You feel guilty every time you choose school over work

A good student job supports your education. It doesn't compete with it for your entire life.

These early work experiences are stepping stones, not your final destination. Every shift teaches you something: how to talk to people, handle stress, manage time, solve problems, and set boundaries.

All of that becomes priceless when you step into internships and full-time roles later.

Next up, we'll build on this foundation and zoom out even further—into the big-picture planning of your professional life after college: networking, internships, and shaping the career you actually want, not just the one you accidentally fall into.

15

Planning Ahead Without Freaking Out About the Future

WHEN EVERYONE ELSE SEEMS AHEAD

Social media definitely makes it worse, but this feeling would exist even without it. You open LinkedIn and see someone from your high school already working at Google. Your roommate lands a fancy internship while you're still trying to figure out what you even *like*.

It feels like everyone has their life together except you.

This feeling is completely normal.

Most people are just better at presenting their wins than sharing their struggles. That person posting about their amazing internship probably applied to fifty companies and got rejected forty-nine times. You just don't see those parts.

Career paths are rarely straight lines. Comparing your behind-the-scenes to someone else's highlight reel will drive you absolutely nuts. Instead of obsessing over where everyone else is, focus on making steady, consistent progress in your own direction.

YOUR TIMELINE DOESN'T HAVE TO MATCH THEIRS

Some people know they want to be doctors at age five and follow that path like a train on a track. Others:

- change majors three times

• take a gap year
• discover their passion in their final semester

Both types of people can end up with successful, fulfilling careers.

The key isn't speed. It's forward momentum.

Here are three totally valid, totally different paths:

• The Direct Route

Florence knew from the start she wanted to be an engineer. She joined engineering clubs, did summer internships, and networked with alumni. By graduation, she already had a job offer lined up. Her path looked efficient and focused.

• The Explorer Route

Daniel started in business, switched to communications, studied abroad, volunteered for a year, and finally discovered nonprofit management in his last year. His winding path gave him adaptability, cultural awareness, and tons of stories that made him stand out in interviews.

• The Practical Route

Priya picked accounting because it seemed stable and "sensible." Along the way, she realized she loved the analytical side more than she expected. Now she works in financial planning, helping people organize their money and hit their goals—and she finds it genuinely satisfying.

None of these paths is "better."

They're just different ways of doing the same thing: building a career that actually fits the person living it.

MAKING PROGRESS WITHOUT PANIC

Instead of spiraling over being "behind," focus on small, doable steps that move you forward.

Explore your interests on purpose. Don't wait for your "calling" to fall from the sky.

• Try different classes
• Go to career panels or employer events
• Ask people how they got into their jobs
• Shadow or volunteer if you can

You can't know what you like without giving yourself things to react to.

. . .

Build skills gradually

Tiny upgrades add up. Over time, improving things like:

- your writing
- your presentation skills
- your basic data/Excel skills
- your ability to talk to strangers without melting

...turns into real, marketable strength.

Document your progress

Keep a running list of:

- projects you've completed
- problems you've solved
- times you stepped up
- compliments or positive feedback you've received

On rough days, looking back at how far you've come is a reality check: you are not as "behind" as your anxiety says you are.

And remember:

Very few people end up exactly where they thought they'd be at eighteen.

That's not a failure. That's just... life.

Your journey is yours. Trust the process.

SKILLS THAT LAUNCH REAL CAREERS

Yes, employers care about your degree. But they care even more about what you can actually do. The good news? You're probably building valuable skills every week without even realizing it.

That group project where one teammate ghosted?

You learned project management and conflict navigation.

That part-time job where you had to explain confusing stuff to annoyed customers?

You built communication and patience.

That dorm fundraiser you helped organize?

You picked up event planning and leadership skills.

Every experience teaches you something transferable—even the ones that felt chaotic at the time.

TECHNICAL SKILLS VS. SOFT SKILLS

Both matter. You don't need to be perfect at everything—you just want a mix.

Technical Skills (job-specific) might include:

- Data analysis and Excel
- Programming languages or specific software
- Lab techniques and research methods
- Adobe Creative Cloud or social media marketing tools
- Accounting systems or financial modeling

Soft Skills (useful literally everywhere):

- Clear written and verbal communication
- Problem-solving under pressure
- Teamwork and collaboration
- Time management and juggling priorities
- Adaptability and learning new things quickly

The most employable grads usually have some technical skills and strong soft skills. Your classes often cover the technical side. Your jobs, clubs, and real-life chaos build the soft stuff.

TRACKING YOUR GROWTH (SO YOU DON'T FORGET IT LATER)

Your brain will absolutely forget the details if you rely on memory alone. Start capturing it now:

Achievement log:

Keep a simple note on your phone or doc titled "Wins." Add things like:

◦ "Led group project, got an A and positive feedback on presentation."

◦ "Handled 50+ customers solo during rush shift when coworker called out."

◦ "Organized fundraiser that raised $600 for local charity."

. . .

Save your work:

Presentations, reports, designs, code, research summaries—anything you might want to show future employers or grad programs.

Collect recommendations early:

When a professor, supervisor, or mentor compliments you, that's your sign to say:

"Thank you—would you be comfortable writing a short recommendation for me in the future?"

Jane worked part-time at a café for three years and thought it "didn't count" for real careers. But when she zoomed out, she saw:

- She trained new hires
- Dealt with long lines and grumpy customers
- Managed inventory when deliveries were late
- Suggested a menu tweak that increased sales by 15%

When she applied for marketing roles, she talked about:

- leadership
- customer experience
- problem-solving
- business awareness

That "just a coffee job" helped her land offers at three different companies.

MAKING YOUR SKILLS VISIBLE

Skills only matter if you can explain them clearly.

Instead of:

"I'm good with people."

Try:

"When customers got frustrated about long wait times, I stayed calm, explained what was happening, and offered solutions—which helped reduce complaints during busy shifts."

Instead of:

"I'm a hard worker."

Try:

"I balanced 15 hours of work a week with a full class schedule and still met all my deadlines."

Use:

- Specific examples
- Concrete results (numbers where you can)
- Language that connects to the job description

Everyone is building their skills at different speeds, in different ways. Your job is not to copy someone else's journey—it's to squeeze as much value as possible out of what you're already doing.

AUTHENTIC CONNECTIONS THAT DON'T FEEL CRINGEY

The word "networking" has big fake-smile, awkward-small-talk energy. But real networking isn't "collecting business cards" or DM-ing strangers like a robot.

It's just:

building real relationships with people who do things you find interesting.

That's it.

The best connections happen when you're genuinely curious, not when you're secretly thinking, "How do I get this person to give me a job?"

STARTING CONVERSATIONS WITHOUT FEELING WEIRD

Shift your mindset from:

- ❌ "What can this person do for me?"

to

- ✅ "What can I learn from this person's experience?"

That's where informational interviews come in. Fancy name, simple idea:

You reach out to someone and say, "Can I ask you about your career and how you got into this field?"

It works because:

- You get real-life insight beyond job descriptions
- They get to share their story (most people like this)
- You build a light, low-pressure connection

When reaching out, make it specific. Instead of:

"I'd love to pick your brain about marketing."

Try:

"I've been following your company's sustainable products campaign, and I'm really curious how you use customer research to shape creative ideas. Would you be open to a short call or coffee chat so I can learn more about your role?"

This shows you cared enough to actually notice what they do, not just copy-paste a generic message.

YOUR UNIVERSITY'S HIDDEN NETWORKING SUPERPOWERS

Your college probably has more resources than you realize (and many students never touch them). Things like:

- Alumni directories
- Formal mentorship programs
- Industry panels and guest speakers
- Employer info sessions
- Career fairs and career center drop-ins

These give you built-in excuses to connect with people—no awkward cold-calls required. You're not "bothering" anyone; the entire system exists for you.

FOLLOWING UP WITHOUT BEING ANNOYING

After you meet someone or have a conversation:

- Send a quick thank-you within a day or two
    - Mention something specific you found helpful
- If they gave advice, update them later if you used it
    - "I took your suggestion and went to that panel—you were right, it was super useful."
- Occasionally send an article, event, or update related to their interests

Aiden didn't know anyone in environmental policy.

He:

1 Attended a university webinar on climate policy

2 Messaged one of the speakers afterward with a thoughtful question

3 That turned into a short call

4 Which led to an invite to a local event

5 Where he met someone who told him about an internship

At no point did it feel like "networking." It just felt like following his curiosity.

The most powerful relationships tend to be the ones that don't feel transactional. Be curious. Be kind. Be human.

PLANNING TOMORROW WHILE FIGHTING TODAY

Here's a secret most adults won't admit:

A lot of them had no idea what they were doing at your age.

Many are still figuring it out.

The job market changes fast. Entire careers appear and disappear in a decade. That's why super rigid five-year plans often fall apart. What matters more is:

- adaptability
- curiosity
- and being willing to learn from wherever you are right now

You do not need a perfect plan to move forward.

FOCUS ON DIRECTION, NOT A FIXED DESTINATION

Instead of, "What do I want to do with my whole life?" (instant panic), try:

"What do I want to learn or explore in the next 6–18 months?"

Ask yourself:

- What kinds of problems do I like solving?
- What activities make me lose track of time (in a good way)?
- What skills do I want to strengthen this year?
- What environments help me do my best work—quiet, busy, structured, flexible?

You don't have to know the final job title. You just need enough direction to choose your next step.

SKILLS THAT TRAVEL WITH YOU EVERYWHERE

No matter where you end up, some skills are always useful:

- Writing clear emails and messages

- Explaining ideas so other people "get it"
- Thinking critically about information
- Managing projects and meeting deadlines
- Using technology and learning new tools quickly
- Working with people who think and communicate differently than you do

You can practice these in:

- group projects
- clubs and leadership roles
- part-time jobs
- volunteering
- even roommate negotiations and house meetings

Nothing is wasted if you're learning from it.

STAYING OPEN TO SURPRISING OPPORTUNITIES

Sometimes the best things happen when your original plan breaks.

Olivia started college dead-set on becoming a lawyer. Halfway through, she realized:

- She dreaded law readings
- But she loved statistics and research methods
- And she cared deeply about social issues

Instead of forcing the law track, she:

- Added a minor in data science
- Looked for research opportunities
- Took on projects that combined data + social impact

She ended up working at a think tank analyzing policy impacts—using:

- her legal knowledge
- her research skills
- and her new data abilities

That career path was *not* in any "What can you do with this major?" pamphlet. It emerged because she was willing to adjust course instead of clinging to the first plan.

MANAGING THE "I'M BEHIND" ANXIETY

It's normal to feel like everyone else is lapping you.

But remember:

- People post their wins, not their panic attacks
- A lot of "put-together" adults are improvising
- There is no single correct timeline

Focus on what you *can* control:

- building useful skills
- collecting varied experiences
- creating real relationships
- paying attention to what energizes you (and what drains you)

The goal isn't to eliminate uncertainty. That's impossible.

The goal is to become the kind of person who can navigate uncertainty with growing confidence—one semester, one decision, one experiment at a time.

Conclusion

When you picked up this book, you might have felt overwhelmed by everything you thought you should already know. Maybe you were stressed about managing money, terrified of signing a lease, or convinced that everyone else had received some secret manual for adulting that somehow skipped you entirely.

Here's the truth: there is no secret manual, and nobody gets handed a complete guide to being an adult on their 18th birthday. What you've been building through this book isn't just a collection of practical skills—it's a foundation for genuine independence. Real independence isn't about never needing help or having all the answers immediately. It's about having the confidence to tackle problems, the knowledge to avoid common pitfalls, and the wisdom to know when to ask for support.

The vision for your adult life isn't perfection—it's competence.

It's being able to look at a bank statement and understand what you're seeing. It's knowing how to have a difficult conversation with a roommate before small annoyances become major conflicts. It's having the basic life skills to take care of yourself while building toward whatever future you want to create.

Every skill you've learned in these pages is a building block toward true independence. Not the kind where you struggle alone and pretend everything's fine, but the kind where you can navigate challenges with confidence, make informed decisions about your money and your life, and build the kind of adult life that feels genuinely yours.

WHAT YOU'VE ACTUALLY ACCOMPLISHED

Financial Literacy Protects Your Future and Opens Doors:

- Understanding the difference between checking and savings accounts, and how to avoid costly banking fees that can drain your resources
- Creating realistic budgets that account for student income sources and help prevent the "it's only $5" spending spirals that derail financial goals
- Building credit responsibly from a young age, avoiding dangerous debt traps like payday loans, and establishing habits that protect your financial future

Good Communication and Organization Solve Most Problems:

- Mastering email etiquette and phone communication skills that work in academic, professional, and personal contexts
- Developing time management systems that work without parental oversight, balancing multiple responsibilities without overwhelming yourself
- Learning conflict resolution scripts and techniques that help address issues with roommates, landlords, and colleagues before they escalate

Basic Life Skills Build Confidence and Save Money:

- Cooking simple, nutritious meals that don't require advanced skills or expensive ingredients, helping you save money and eat better than surviving on takeaways
- Managing laundry, cleaning, and basic home maintenance to avoid costly mistakes and create a living space you actually want to spend time in

- Understanding leases, tenant rights, and how to interact with landlords to protect yourself from housing disputes and financial losses

THE MOST IMPORTANT LESSONS

Everyone Learns Adulting Gradually - You're Not Behind:

The biggest lie about adulthood is that everyone else figured it out faster than you did. Florence thought she was the only one who didn't know how to read a lease until her friend admitted she'd been too embarrassed to ask what "joint and several liability" meant. Cole felt like an idiot for not understanding credit scores until he realized his older brother had made costly mistakes with credit cards that took years to fix.

The truth is that most people learn these skills through trial and error, often making expensive mistakes along the way. By learning them systematically, you're actually ahead of the curve.

Small, Consistent Actions Build Major Life Skills:

Adulting isn't about dramatic transformations or perfect execution from day one. It's about small, consistent habits that compound over time. Checking your bank balance weekly prevents overdraft fees. Cleaning your kitchen after cooking prevents overwhelming deep-cleaning sessions. Responding to emails within 24 hours builds a reputation for reliability.

These tiny actions might seem insignificant in the moment, but they create the foundation for a well-managed adult life.

Confidence Comes from Competence and Practice:

Adult confidence isn't about feeling fearless—it's about knowing you can handle whatever comes up. When you understand how your bank account works, you approach financial decisions with clarity rather than anxiety. When you know how to have difficult conversations, you can address problems directly instead of avoiding them until they explode.

This competence-based confidence is much more reliable than bravado or wishful thinking. It's built through repeated practice in low-stakes situations, so when high-stakes moments arise, you have proven skills to draw upon.

YOUR NEXT STEPS

Start with One Skill Area That Feels Most Urgent:

Look back through the chapters and identify which area feels most pressing for your current situation. Are you moving into your first rental and need to focus on housing skills? Is money stress keeping you up at night, suggesting you should start with budgeting basics? Choose one area and commit to mastering those basics before moving on.

Use the Checklists and Scripts as Training Wheels:

Don't try to memorize everything or wing it based on general principles. Use the specific checklists when viewing apartments, the email templates when communicating with professors or landlords, and the conversation scripts when making phone calls or addressing conflicts. These tools aren't crutches—they're training wheels that help you build skills safely.

Practice New Skills in Low-Stakes Situations First:

Before you need to have a serious conversation with your landlord about a broken heating system, practice professional communication by emailing professors about office hours or assignment clarifications. Before you're responsible for cooking all your meals, try making one simple dish per week while you still have backup food options.

This approach lets you refine your skills when mistakes are less costly and builds muscle memory for when the stakes are higher.

A FINAL TRUTH

Here's what I want you to remember on the days when adulting feels impossible: every competent adult you admire was once exactly where you are now. They've all sent emails they immediately regretted, made financial mistakes that kept them awake at night, and stood in grocery stores feeling overwhelmed by choices.

The difference between thriving adults and those who struggle isn't that the successful ones never felt lost or made mistakes. It's that they kept learning, kept practicing, and gradually built the skills and confidence that make adult life manageable and even enjoyable.

By working through this book, you've already demonstrated

something crucial: you're willing to learn rather than just hoping things will work out.

That mindset—the willingness to learn, practice, and gradually improve—is the most important adult skill of all. Everything else is just details.

You're going to make mistakes. You're going to have days when you feel like you're barely keeping up. You're going to encounter situations this book didn't cover, and you'll have to figure things out as you go.

That's not a sign that you're failing at adulting—that's exactly what adulting looks like for everyone.

But you're also going to have moments of genuine pride when you handle a difficult situation with confidence, when you realize you've developed skills that help friends and family, when you look around your space and realize you've created a life that feels authentically yours.

The skills in this book are your foundation, but your adult life will be your own creation. Use what works, adapt what doesn't, and keep building on what you've learned here.

You're more capable than you think, more resilient than you know, and more ready for independence than you feel right now.

Go build the adult life you want. You've got this.

Bonuses

This book includes free bonus resources to help you put these skills into action. To keep the book more portable and reduce page count, the extras are provided digitally. Simply scan the QR code printed below to access your downloads, checklists, and practical tools anytime.

www.ingramcontent.com/pod-product-compliance
Lightning Source LLC
Chambersburg PA
CBHW071451070426
42452CB00039B/1035

* 9 7 8 1 0 6 8 4 9 0 7 9 8 *